MW01026044

A Guide to
Pentecostal Movements
for Lutherans

A Guide to
Pentecostal Movements
for Lutherans

Sarah Hinlicky Wilson

FOREWORD BY
Jean-Daniel Plüss

WIPF & STOCK · Eugene, Oregon

INSTITUTE FOR ECUMENICAL RESEARCH · Strasbourg, France

A GUIDE TO PENTECOSTAL MOVEMENTS FOR LUTHERANS

Wipf & Stock
An Imprint of Wipf and Stock Publishers
199 W. 8th Ave., Suite 3
Eugene, OR 97401

www.wipfandstock.com

PAPERBACK ISBN: 978-1-4982-8985-6
HARDCOVER ISBN: 978-1-4982-8987-0
EBOOK ISBN: 978-1-4982-8986-3

Manufactured in the U.S.A.

Contents

Foreword

IN 2008 WHEN I first met Sarah Hinlicky Wilson on a cold December day
in Zürich, Switzerland, I encountered a person who was willing to get
into a discussion. We had been invited to talks on our respective views of
our traditions, Pentecostal and Lutheran. Like the weather, the situation
was at first a bit frosty, as if the world of Lutherans and that of Classical
Pentecostals were like two continents still drifting apart. So no wonder if
the conversations would be careful and characterized by a certain distance.

Eight years have since passed and we have come to appreciate our
common Christian faith—we have become friends without having to aban-
don our basic beliefs and religious roots. Sarah has studied Pentecostalism
in great detail and has now written this book, testifying to the ecumenical
importance of nursing conversations between Lutherans and Pentecostals.
This book is being published at a time when official dialogue between the
Lutherans World Federation and Classical Pentecostals is about to begin.

Besides introducing the reader to both the Pentecostal movement and
the Lutheran confession, she addresses major issues that arise when the two
groups talk together. Do we have a common understanding of baptism?
How can we understand the role of charisms in the church? But she does
not stop at clarifying theological ideas. With her avid mind she addresses
hermeneutical issues as well. What can we learn from our respective histories and how do these influence our judgment? She then moves on to
discussing touchy issues: the function of power in Pentecostal circles, the
influence of prosperity teaching, and the role of experience in faith and
religious life. Now conversations can begin and contacts can be fostered.
Both will hopefully strengthen the life of the church and ultimately give
glory to God.

The reader will find that Sarah Hinlicky Wilson is not only a keen
observer and a fair commentator, but also a person with a pastoral vision.

However, the book's title could be somewhat misleading. The book is not just a guide to Pentecostalism for Lutherans; it is also a well-written text that can challenge Pentecostals to understand how other Christians see them. As such her work serves a double purpose.

Jean-Daniel Plüss

Co-Chair
Lutheran World Federation–
Classical Pentecostal Dialogue

Acknowledgments

ECUMENICAL EFFORTS ARE BY definition collaborative. This book could not have been written without the support, wisdom, and assistance of many people.

My colleagues at the Institute for Ecumenical Research—Theodor Dieter, André Birmelé, and Elisabeth Parmentier—modeled for me a more excellent way in ecumenism than I had ever imagined possible before I met them. I am grateful for their eloquent fidelity to Lutheran theology as well as their open and knowledgeable engagement with the whole range of other Christian traditions. I am also thankful for the always capable and kindly help of Elke Leypold, the Institute's administrative assistant, and Sylvie Speckel, the Institute's librarian. Kenneth Appold, who preceded me at the Institute and continues as adjunct professor, initiated the Institute's dialogue with Classical Pentecostals. It was through one of these gatherings that I first became acquainted with, and then intrigued and fascinated by, the Pentecostal movement worldwide. I wish to express my gratitude to him for opening up this new conversation among divided Christians, as well as to the Pentecostal participants who so patiently answered my countless questions. I am particularly grateful to Cecil M. Robeck Jr. and Jean-Daniel Plüss for their continuing friendship, and additionally to Jean-Daniel for reading and critiquing this book and for writing such an encouraging preface.

The point of this book, however, is not to remain within the small circle of professional ecumenists but to make our work fruitful for a wide audience of Christians concerned with the issues addressed herein. Therefore I turned to readers around the world, lay and clergy, to read this book and make suggestions for its improvement. I can attest that the book is much improved for their comments, and any remaining errors or misjudgments should be attributed to me, not to them. My deepest thanks to these readers: in the United States, Troy M. Troftgruben, Cheryl M. Peterson, Robert C. Saler, and Paul R. Hinlicky; in Brazil, Eric P. Nelson; in Germany/France, Theodor Dieter; in Estonia, Annely Neame; in Finland, Sammeli Juntunen; in Tanzania, Nehemia Moshi; in South Korea, Jin-Seop Eom; and in Australia, Victor C. Pfitzner.

Introduction

IT MIGHT STRIKE YOU as strange that this little book about Pentecostal movements, written for Lutherans, is called a "guide." It sounds like something you might take along on a trip to a foreign land. But that is exactly what is intended.

A guide is not the usual way of informing one set of Christians about another. What you will find here is not a history or theology of Pentecostalism written by a Pentecostal, either for committed Pentecostals or to persuade outsiders. Nor is it an analysis and critique of Pentecostalism according to typical Lutheran criteria, evaluating how well Pentecostals do at being Lutheran.

It is much more an account by a Lutheran who has done some journeying among Pentecostals and Charismatics through both reading and personal experience. I first came to work with Pentecostals by joining the "proto-dialogue" between Lutherans and Pentecostals that began under the auspices of the Institute for Ecumenical Research in Strasbourg, France. As an ecumenist, therefore, I try to represent Pentecostalism as accurately and fairly as possible. A skewed or hostile guide wouldn't help you make your own journey and would probably deter you from making such a journey at all! But because the journey has been made by a Lutheran, who has been trained to interpret and react to things in a certain way, it definitely reflects Lutherans interests, questions, and concerns—perhaps in ways that would surprise Pentecostal onlookers. My hope is that an account by a Lutheran who has made this trip will embolden other Lutherans to do the same, to understand what they are seeing, and to learn from the experience.

A rewarding travel experience does two things. First, it shows us how other human beings live: how they eat, how they dress, how they celebrate, how they work, how they organize their lives together. Such an experience expands our own understanding of the range of human experience, good and bad alike. Second, travel makes us see our own home in a new light. What was once taken to be normal and universal is now perceived to be local and particular. Of course there are universals—but we can't actually know what the universals are until we have seen them embodied in different particulars. The travel experience helps us sort out which is which.

In this guide, however, there is much more than common humanity to unite what is foreign with what is familiar. The most essential thing that Pentecostals and Lutherans have in common is we are all baptized Christians, believers in the crucified and risen Jesus, called by the gospel to new life. There is only so "foreign" we can be to one another if we all call Jesus our brother and our Lord! To be one church, under one Lord, through one baptism, is a consequence of the gospel. As Ephesians 2:14 puts it, "For he himself is our peace, who has made us both one and has broken down in his flesh the dividing wall of hostility."

We know, however, through the long and sad tale of church history, that Christians have tended to value their differences more than their commonalities. We have tended to put a premium on the things that divide us and have given less weight to the things that unite us. But a church that lives by division dies by division. A habit of excluding other Christians will eventually circle back home and cause internal division as well. Churches don't flourish when there are high and thick walls built around them. In the real life of a church, the boundaries are fluid. There is overlap between churches as well as distinctions between them.

The purpose of this guide, then, is not to establish once and for all what is held in common and what remains different between Pentecostals and Lutherans—much less to maintain those differences forever and ever. It is rather to assist Lutherans in the task of faithfully recognizing the work of God wherever it may found and acknowledging Pentecostals as our sisters and brothers in Christ. Because we are already one in Christ, therefore we must learn to live together as one. Only if we start from the assumption that we are one body in Christ can our critiques, challenges, and appreciations of one another become fruitful. Only in this way can we attempt joint worship and prayer, shared diaconal work and political activity, teach one another and learn from one another. Only in this way can our unity become visible to the world.

It should further be noted at the outset that I am not only a traveler from Lutheranism to Pentecostalism but also a traveler from America who has spent a significant amount of time in Europe, with some short visits to the other parts of the world. In some ways that is an advantage. The most influential form of Pentecostalism arose in the United States and continues to exercise its influence around the world, so I as an American have a certain familiarity with Pentecostalism's home territory. I have tried to cast a wide net in this book, to draw in the experiences and histories of other parts of the world, but I can't escape the American lenses that I bring to what I see. This also means that the Lutheranism I know best is that of the North Atlantic world. It is inevitable that I will sometimes seem to be speaking primarily as one North Atlantic Lutheran to another, though here too I have tried to take a broader perspective into account. I ask the reader's patience when my perspective seems to darken rather than enlighten. In any event, I repeat: I am not trying to offer the final word on this subject. I encourage you, the reader, to undertake your own ecumenical journeys, wherever you are. I would be very glad to hear your report!

A word of both warning and encouragement before you set out. Ecumenical travel experiences, like any other travel experiences, are unsettling. They call into question what you have always taken for granted. They impose spiritual humility and force you to ask whether you have understood and lived as well as you might have. Hearing another account of what it means to be a Christian might make you angry; it might make you frightened; it might make you feel lost or confused. Be assured, that is entirely normal. If you stay with it, you will come out the other side a more faithful disciple of Jesus Christ. The challenge will deliver back to you the faith you have always had, but purified, stronger, and wiser.

CHAPTER 1

Azusa

The news has spread far and wide that Los Angeles is being visited
with a "rushing mighty wind from heaven." The how and why of it
is to be found in the very opposite of those conditions that are usually thought necessary for a big revival. No instruments of music
are used, none are needed. No choir, but bands of angels have been
heard by some in the Spirit and there is a heavenly singing that is
inspired by the Holy Ghost. No collections are taken. No bills have
been posted to advertise the meetings. No church or organization
is at the back of it. All who are in touch with God realize as soon
as they enter the meetings that the Holy Ghost is the leader. One
brother stated that even before his train entered the city, he felt the
power of the revival.[1]

THIS IS HOW *The Apostolic Faith*, the newspaper published by the Azusa
Street Mission in Los Angeles, California, described the sudden outburst
of spiritual gifts and gospel passion among its people in April 1906. But
that's not how the secular newspapers described it. The journalists saw only
the mad antics of "holy rollers" and the indecent blurring of color lines as
blacks laid hands on whites and prayed for them to receive the Holy Spirit.
Ever since, the meaning of the Azusa Street revival has been disputed, not
only between its proponents and skeptical critics, but between different
groups of Christians as well.

How did such an extraordinary revival come about with so little of the
usual preparation, as the newspaper quotation testifies? What did people
see in the plain wooden building in an unprepossessing neighborhood of
Los Angeles? Why was the ministry of William J. Seymour (1870–1922) so
unprecedentedly effective at fostering the growth of spiritual gifts and commitment to mission at home and abroad? How did it happen that the little

1. Quoted in Robeck, *The Azusa Street Mission and Revival*, 52.

Azusa Street Mission became synonymous with the rise of Pentecostalism, a movement that now claims half a billion members or more?

To start answering these questions, we need to back up a bit and take a look at nineteenth-century American Christianity.

During this period, despite the presence of all kinds of Christians in America as well as people with no Christian convictions at all, the dominant theology was Methodist, as formulated by the eighteenth-century itinerant English preacher John Wesley (1703–1791). Even non-Methodist churches with no apparent fondness for Methodist theology, like the Reformed, were deeply influenced by it. The early part of the nineteenth century was marked by what is called the Second Great Awakening: a time of renewed religious commitment, camp meetings, tent revivals, dramatic conversions, emotional repentance, and intense hopes for the future. (The First Great Awakening, in the eighteenth century, took place in the northeastern part of the country and mainly involved people who were already church members.) Many believed that the return of Christ in judgment was imminent and that the millennium-long reign of his saints was on the way. The arrival of the eschaton was intensely desired.

The mood of American Christianity was optimistic. It believed in the perfectibility of the Christian, a conviction inherited from Wesley as explained in his treatise, *A Brief Account of Christian Perfection*. This teaching was given a renewed American impetus by Asa Mahan (1799–1889), college president and author of *The Scripture Doctrine of Christian Perfection*, and by revivalist preacher Phoebe Palmer (1807–1874). For them, it was not enough to say that sin had been forgiven. Methodist doctrine taught that the dominion of sin over the believer could be fully destroyed; that the inclination to sin could be conquered. Early nineteenth-century American Christianity likewise believed in the perfectibility of human society, giving rise to all kinds of reform movements toward temperance, the abolition of slavery, and education. Many people believed that God would not withhold any good thing from His children if they earnestly desired and prayed for it, sinlessness included. Holiness churches, an offshoot of Methodism, grew in size and importance as they promoted these teachings.

It is important to note that the assumption of this kind of Christianity is one of adult conversion. The ancient civilizations and folk churches of the Middle East and Europe, where Christianity was so fully incorporated into the life of the society that the baptism of infants was often required by law, no longer made any sense on the American frontier. Colonial American culture was one without ancient institutions, intoxicated by the opportunity for a fresh start, based on personal commitment and decision rather than law or custom. Baptism, therefore, was understood to be the result of a conscious adult experience of regeneration by God. Baptism was not primarily a church ritual or an act of God but a public witness to an internal spiritual event. (The Lutheran Confessions also speak frequently of regeneration, but they assume it will be subsequent to, and in part the result of, baptism, which in the sixteenth-century European context was nearly always infant baptism.)

But following the Methodist line of thought, it was not enough to turn to God in faith at regeneration. Wesley's logic was simple: God wants us to love Him completely, and God can accomplish what He intends. Why should we assume that we convert to Christ only to be continually defeated by sin? God can conquer the sin in us, even now upon this earth. Thus the Holiness movement came more and more to emphasize a "second work of grace" after justification or conversion, which they called "entire sanctification." Whereas Reformed and Lutheran Protestants understood sanctification to be a gradual, lifelong process to be completed only at the resurrection of the dead, Holiness Christians understood it to be as instantaneous and experiential as conversion itself.

The optimistic mood of American Christianity was well matched by the growth of both science and industry, but it didn't last as long as the other two. The biggest and bitterest blow was the American Civil War (1861–1865). Approximately 620,000 people lost their lives in this conflict—which was 2 percent of the entire American population at the time—and that on top of four hundred years of the enslavement and horrific maltreatment of persons of African descent. By the time it was all over, even the most fervent Christian had a hard time expecting the best of the human race. And yet the hopes of decades past didn't simply dry up and disappear. Other explanations were sought and, above all, deeper experiences of God.

Around the turn of the twentieth century, a new teaching began to make the rounds in Holiness churches. Benjamin Hardin Irwin (1854–c. 1920s) had experienced both regeneration and entire sanctification, but during his preaching journeys he had a third experience, which he called a "baptism by fire" or "baptism in the Holy Spirit." The believers that gathered around him accordingly called themselves the Fire-Baptized movement. Most Holiness churches quickly rejected Irwin and his "third work" teaching. Indeed, due to his excessively creative ideas about "dynamite," "lyddite," and "oxidite" baptisms, plus a moral scandal, he fell from the radar and died in obscurity. Still, his notion of a "third blessing" or "third experience of grace" after conversion and sanctification began to gain ground. The third blessing idea was particularly vital in such denominations as the Church of God (Cleveland, Tennessee) and the Pentecostal Holiness Church, with which the Fire-Baptized churches eventually merged. At this point in time, though, "Pentecostal" did not yet mean what we mean by it today.

Then another person came on the scene: Charles Fox Parham (1873–1929). He started out as a preacher in a Methodist church but in time was attracted to Holiness teaching. He eventually struck out on his own with a ministry of divine healing—another prominent theme of nineteenth-century American Christianity. During a visit to a Holiness commune in the northeastern United States, Parham heard about missionaries who had received xenolalia: the miraculous gift of speech in a foreign language, akin to what took place on the day of Pentecost in Acts 2. (Xenolalia is to be distinguished from glossolalia, which is speech in the tongues "of angels" or otherwise incomprehensible speech.)

Suddenly all the pieces fell into place for Parham. If you could speak a foreign language, you could instantly become a missionary. Jesus had said that the gospel must first be preached to all nations (Mark 13:10), and once that had happened he would come again in glory (13:26). If xenolalia was being bestowed upon believers, it must be in preparation for the final missionary push and, therefore, the end times. It was not simply a private experience of edification but an equipping for service.

Parham opened a school in Topeka, Kansas, in the American heartland, where he challenged his students to find hard-and-fast proof of Spirit baptism. Plenty of people in Holiness circles by now were talking of being baptized in the Spirit, which they equated with the second work of grace, namely entire sanctification. But Parham and his students together became convinced that speaking in tongues was *the* proof of baptism in the Spirit, or, as it was later doctrinally defined by the newborn Pentecostal churches, tongues was the "initial evidence" or "initial physical evidence" or "Bible evidence" of Spirit baptism. A search for absolute certainty—whether of salvation, sanctification, or anything else—was a longstanding theme in American Christianity, and evidential tongues accompanying Spirit baptism fit neatly into the pattern. Parham and his students started praying for the gift, and on January 1, 1901, one of the students, Agnes Ozman, spoke in tongues. The same happened to Parham himself and about half the other students over the next few days. Despite Parham's passionate evangelistic efforts, though, few people joined them, and the Apostolic Faith movement, as he called it, languished in obscurity for some time.

A few years later the movement began to pick up again, though at its height it never had more than ten thousand members. Internal conflict also began to fester, and other leaders soon eclipsed Parham. A probably false accusation of moral misdeeds sealed his fate. But what limited his reach most was his unchangeable conviction that the gift of tongues was always xenolalia. The problem was that, almost without exception, Spirit-baptized missionaries quickly discovered they'd been mistaken about their ability to speak in foreign languages! Whatever they were speaking, it wasn't a known foreign language.

The main reason Parham is remembered today is because of William J. Seymour, the aforementioned preacher of Azusa Street. Seymour had grown up in the largely Catholic world of Louisiana, the son of ex-slaves. As an adult he traveled north in search of work and became involved with Methodist Episcopal and Evening Light Saints churches. He was a premillennialist awaiting the imminent return of Christ, and a believer in "special revelation"—probably inherited from slave Christianity—meaning divine direction granted through dreams, visions, voices, and trances. This did *not* mean, however, additions to the revelation granted in Holy Scripture. All such special revelations were to be tested against the Bible and repudiated if found to be at odds with it.

In the course of his wanderings, Seymour came to Parham's school looking for answers to his religious questions. Parham, an avowed racist, would only allow Seymour to sit in the hallway and listen; the black man couldn't be in the same room as everyone else.

Despite the discrimination, Seymour listened attentively and took Parham seriously. He himself had experienced entire sanctification and believed, like most other Holiness Christians, that this experience had included baptism in the Spirit. It seemed only logical: how could you be entirely sanctified *without* having been baptized in the Spirit? But then, Christ himself was entirely sinless and yet he also needed to be baptized in the Spirit—and that, significantly, was the inauguration of his ministry. Holiness stressed perfection and cleansing, but it said little of missionary power and equipping. That was the missing piece. Seymour was convinced, but he himself had not yet received what was now being called the "third blessing" when he left Parham's company.

In 1906, while still studying at Parham's school, Seymour received an invitation to become the pastor of a Holiness church in California. He arrived in Los Angeles in February of that year and started teaching that baptism in the Spirit was an equipping for ministry, not a gift of purity or sanctification—that, in fact, it was a third work of grace. Saying so got him promptly locked out of the church. Those who'd invited him in the first place came to regard him as a heretic.

But another family in the congregation had mercy on Seymour and took him in. At a Bible study hosted by the family, he continued to teach that there were three works of grace, and that baptism in the Spirit only followed upon the first two works of conversion and sanctification. This eventually became known as the doctrine of subsequence: an important affirmation that sanctification and Spirit-baptism are not the *cause* but the *result* of salvation, and that all three are the work of God. Believers could pray for Spirit-baptism, tarry for it (long periods of prayer and worship with other believers), and yearn for it, but God was the one who gave it. They would know when they'd received it—it was not a silent or unnoticed kind of event—and the proof would be speaking in tongues. Seymour crucially differed from Parham on the nature of these tongues: he believed they were not xenolalia, as in Acts 2, but glossolalia, as in I Corinthians 14. The distinction between sanctification and Spirit-baptism, and understanding the latter as an empowerment for mission, is what set Seymour's teaching apart from the classical Holiness position. And this is what came to be defined as specifically Pentecostal.

In April, Seymour's teaching came rapidly and dramatically to flower. Participants in the Bible study began to speak in tongues. A few days later, Seymour himself finally did too. Almost at once visitors came to see what was happening, and within a week it became necessary to rent the space on Azusa Street.

The Mission was soon abuzz with activity. There were Bible studies every day, prayer meetings in people's homes and in camps outside the city, local evangelistic outreach, and of course frequent worship. The worship style was in the classic African-American pattern of call-and-response preaching and impassioned singing and prayer. Mark 16 and Acts 2:4 were favorite texts of Seymour's, and he quoted Isaiah more than any other book of the Bible. The Lord's Supper was celebrated often, as was foot-washing, another Holiness distinctive. Baptism was performed by full immersion in the name of the Father, the Son, and the Holy Spirit. Speaking and singing in tongues were both common, as were more unusual signs of having fallen under the Spirit's power, such as trances and dancing. These were the sorts of things that drew the scorn of the secular press, but they equally drew seekers from all races and all social classes. Women were as active in Azusa's ministry as men. Long-term Christians and seasoned clergy were as attracted to the revival as those who were not yet baptized believers. The sheer fact of a racially integrated congregation was a miracle at that period in American history.

Seymour's leadership was nothing short of extraordinary. He struck a balance that was nicely expressed in the mission's newspaper: "If there is too much reading of the Word without prayer, you get too argumentative, and if you pray too much without reading, you get fanatical."[2] Seymour taught the tripartite conversion-sanctification-Spirit baptism pattern, but his orientation was always obedience to God, not the accomplishment of religious phenomena. "Do not seek for tongues," he said, "but for the promise of the Father, and pray for the baptism with the Holy Ghost, and God will throw in the tongues according to Acts 2:4."[3]

Though he preached regularly, Seymour deliberately made room for lay leadership and even for competing and dissenting voices. One visitor actually got up to denounce the whole revival and in the very process found himself being converted! While Seymour was well aware of the mixed motives of the human heart and insisted on regular scriptural discernment of all developments, he equally recognized the need to trust and nourish other Christians in their own callings. The result was that, while only fifty to sixty people formed the long-term core of the congregation, thousands more passed through the Mission and in so doing heard their own call to Christian ministry. Countless people departed Azusa Street directly for points overseas and devoted their entire lives to global mission.

Despite Seymour's irenic and humble approach to ministry, the Azusa Street Mission was not without conflict. Quite the contrary. Charles Parham visited about six months after the revival got underway and was downright horrified by what he saw. Undoubtedly spurred by his racist dislike of the African-American character of the worship, especially the more demonstrative aspects of it, he tried to stage a takeover of the Mission. The

2. Quoted in Robeck, *The Azusa Street Mission and Revival*, 142.
3. Quoted in Robeck, *The Azusa Street Mission and Revival*, 163.

regulars wouldn't hear of it, so Parham opened his own competing church nearby, to little success.

Two years later, probably due to jealousy over Seymour's marriage, one of the Azusa Street leaders named Clara Lum absconded with most of the equipment and the mailing list for *The Apostolic Faith* and set up her own Pentecostal mission in Portland, Oregon, along with another former member. All of Seymour's efforts to regain control of his newspaper failed, and he ended up being sidelined during the explosive growth of the Pentecostal movement over the next few years.

Then in 1911, during one of Seymour's preaching tours away from home, a Chicago pastor named William H. Durham (1873–1936) was invited to preach in his absence. Durham had visited Azusa before and received the baptism in the Spirit while he was there. Seymour even prophesied on that occasion that wherever Durham went he would cause the Holy Spirit to fall upon the gathered people. But by the time he returned as a guest preacher, Durham had made a major break with classical Holiness teaching. He no longer accepted the "second work of grace," namely entire sanctification. Instead, he argued, the "Finished Work" of Christ on the cross made all of the savior's holiness available to Christians immediately at the moment of conversion. What Christ accomplished would and must be continually appropriated by the Christian over the course of life, rather than all in a single experienced moment. Durham preached this message during his visit to Azusa, but his real goal was to take over the Mission. Seymour came home early, and this time he was the one to lock out a preacher with an unacceptable message. Durham responded by starting his own mission a few blocks away, just as Parham had.

As if that weren't enough, in 1913 a camp meeting took place at nearby Arroyo Seco under the auspices of the Mission but without inviting Seymour, and at that meeting someone prophesied that Christians should baptize only in the name of Jesus, as was done in the Book of Acts, not in the trinitarian name. This practice soon spread far and wide. Before long it was accompanied by a denial of the Trinity, claiming that Jesus alone was God. Spirit baptism was equated with both conversion *and* sanctification— it was one single salvific experience. This proved to be the most permanent and destructive split in the nascent Pentecostal movement. Those who followed the new teaching were called Oneness or Jesus' Name Pentecostals.

The Azusa Street revival lasted only about three years, from 1906 to 1909. It saw a brief flare-up again in the second decade of the twentieth century, but by the time of Seymour's death in 1922 it was marginal. In the meanwhile, Seymour had seen enough to modify his own teachings somewhat. He no longer considered tongues alone to be sufficient Bible evidence of baptism in the Spirit: a person also had to be immersed in the love of God and display the spiritual fruit of love in daily life. The washing away of the color line, which had always been important to Seymour, was one of the most important signs of the genuine work of the Spirit and the gift of love.

Despite the short duration of the revival and the ultimate inconsequence of the Azusa Street Mission to the rapidly growing Pentecostal churches, there is no doubt that Seymour and his congregation made an unprecedentedly enormous impact on world Christianity. There is almost no better example of how God uses the humble and insignificant to accomplish great things.

For Further Reading

Cecil M. Robeck Jr., *The Azusa Street Mission and Revival: The Birth of the Global Pentecostal Movement* (Nashville: Thomas Nelson, 2006).

CHAPTER 2

Pentecostals

IT WOULD BE NEAT and tidy if the previous chapter described the origin of the Pentecostal movement and its founder. But it doesn't. The story of Azusa Street is the beginning of our book because it is so famous, so influential, and so representative. But it is neither the origin nor the epicenter of Pentecostalism. In fact, it is quite difficult to pinpoint just what the origin might be.

We have already heard about Charles Parham, another contender for the claim to be the source or founder of Pentecostalism. But long before his students discovered and experienced the "Bible evidence" for baptism in the Spirit, Pentecostal awakenings were taking place in India. The deep roots of these revivals were the Pietist missions of the early nineteenth century (including Lutheran missionaries Wilhelm Ringeltaube and Carl Rhenius), which favored indigenous self-support and leadership instead of the paternalistic control of new churches by old ones.

The first Indian revival took place in 1860 in Tirunelveli in the present-day state of Tamil Nadu. It was led by an Anglican Englishman, John Christian Aroolappen, but quickly became fully Indian in leadership and practice. There were prophecies, speaking in tongues, outbursts of repentance, visions, dreams, and being slain in the Spirit. Church offices found in the New Testament but absent from historic churches were revived: apostle, prophet, and evangelist. Women became key leaders and evangelists as well as men. And it was all accomplished without Western money or control, which at that time was nearly unheard of. The number of conversions was impressive. Gradually the Tirunelveli revival spread to Travancore in today's Kerala state, which gave rise to the second awakening in India in 1874 and 1875. Along with all the other dramatic spiritual gifts, the caste line was eliminated among participants—foreshadowing Seymour's conviction about baptism in the Spirit washing away the color line in America.

The legacy of these revivals was itself revived when news came to India of the Welsh revival in 1905 (of which more in a moment). In June a young Indian girl experienced the "baptism by fire" and once again what we now call Pentecostal phenomena began to spread throughout the country. This time, more Western missionaries participated in the movement, most significantly a Methodist woman named Minnie F. Abrams (1859–1912). She wrote an influential account of the events in her book *Baptism in the Holy Ghost and Fire*, where she emphasized both purification and missionary empowerment. Azusa Street missionaries eventually arrived in India too, and in time denominations were formed that took on some of the flavor of American Pentecostalism. But it is important to note that the experience of the outpouring of the Spirit and divine gifts had been known in India much earlier than in America, and further, that Indians by and large did not see glossolalia as the necessary evidence of baptism in the Spirit.

Then there was the aforementioned revival of 1904 and 1905 that took place in Wales, in the western part of Great Britain. Here again glossolalia was not treated as evidence of baptism in the Spirit—indeed, there was little or nothing taught of such a "third work" at all—but the revival was certainly characterized by spiritual gifts, prophecy, singing in the Spirit, passionate prayer, and emotional outpourings. It is notable that here also an emphasis was laid on indigenous cultural forms of worship that had otherwise been suppressed by the official churches. News of the Welsh revival inspired many of the Americans who later got involved in the Azusa Street Mission, and historically it has been regarded as a John the Baptist-type preparation for Pentecostalism. Most early British Pentecostals had some connection to the Welsh revival, too.

Chile was another center of Pentecostal revival independent of what was happening in Los Angeles. An American Methodist missionary got hold of Minnie Abrams's book on the revival in India and was so moved by what he read that he sought the baptism in the Spirit—after first asking permission from his congregation. In due time this pastor, Willis Hoover (1858–1936), received what he'd prayed for, and immediately thereafter a revival broke out in his church, starting in September 1909. It spread beyond the bounds of Methodism (and, in fact, the Methodist church forced Hoover to resign) and gave birth to one of the earliest Pentecostal denominations, the Iglesia Metodista Pentecostal. It should come as no surprise by now that it cultivated distinctively Chilean elements in its worship and order and did not teach tongues as initial evidence.

Another significant revival took place in Korea around this time. Western missionaries of different denominations had been gathering for prayer and repentance, reflecting on their failures to communicate the gospel successfully to Koreans. News came of the revivals in India, Wales, and Azusa Street. In early 1907, a gathering of Methodists and Presbyterians was overcome by a mysterious presence, which stayed with them and drew Westerners and Koreans alike to their meetings. This presence of God inspired profound, sustained repentance and incredible thirst for the Word of God. People would walk for hours or days to attend Bible studies. They would rise very early in the morning to gather for prayer, a habit that characterizes Korean Christianity to this day. The revival ultimately overcame the dividing wall between missionary and indigenous Christians.

And while detailed historical study still remains to be done, some scholars estimate that by 1900 there were as many as one million African Christians with all the typical signs of Pentecostal practice.

What makes the Azusa Street Mission worthy of special attention is *not* that it was the first or the center. Rather, it's that Azusa transformed the initial Pentecostal revivals from something basically local and unconnected to something truly transnational. The explosive growth and universal reach of Pentecostalism became a reality after Azusa, not before. But because there has never been any central control, even at its most global Pentecostalism has always been locally adapted. This makes generalizations about it exceedingly difficult.

After even this brief historical overview, it should be clear how inappropriate and unhelpful it is to try set up a one-to-one comparison between the Reformation, from which Lutherans draw their theological identity, and the Pentecostal revivals. The Lutheran Reformation took place in a much more homogenous religious environment than any of the Pentecostal revivals; its origins were in the university; it had a single founder who also became the dominant theologian and leader of the movement; it had major conflicts with political powers and ended up having to take its own political stands. (It should be remembered, however, that there were other Reformations by other reformers who had other values, so that the Reformation *overall* was quite diverse.) By contrast, Pentecostalism has had multiple "centers"; it has had no single theologian or leader who has spoken for the whole; it has arisen in wildly different social realities, from fervent but divided Christendom to places where Christianity is a tiny minority; and it has never had or used political force to back it up—in fact, most early

American Pentecostals were pacifists. And with so many different varieties of Pentecostalism, it isn't particularly helpful to equate Pentecostals with "Enthusiasts," as many Lutherans instinctively do. For this reason, we won't return to the question of Enthusiasm until the final chapter of this book, where we'll deal with the topic of experience.

It is further important to note that Pentecostal controversies did not, by and large, pertain to salvation or ecclesiology to the same degree that they did in the Lutheran Reformation. The distinctive Pentecostal question is rather what believers can expect of their lives *after* conversion or salvation.

Altogether this makes identifying Pentecostals much trickier business than it is with Lutherans or other members of "historic" churches. There is no defining confessional document or theological writing, other than the Bible, that is universally accepted by all Pentecostals. Nor is there any single structure or type of church government that defines them—among Pentecostals you will find everything from independent lay-led congregations to episcopal hierarchies. Even the order and style of worship will vary from place to place, from spontaneous participatory liturgies to tightly controlled performances.

For our purposes here, we will use this working definition of Pentecostalism: *a movement to reclaim experience of the Holy Spirit and such spiritual gifts as tongues, prophecy, and healing as a normal part of every Christian's life.* This is a deliberately broad definition. We'll turn now to take a look at the major subdivisions within Pentecostalism.

Classical Trinitarian Pentecostals. At just over a hundred years old, there is already a variety of Pentecostalism known as "classical"! These are the denominations that emerged from the revivals in America in the early twentieth century.

The first churches to accept Pentecostal theology and practice were originally Holiness denominations that came to accept the "third work" teaching about baptism in the Spirit. These are, for example, the Pentecostal Holiness Church, the Church of God (Cleveland, Tennessee), and the Church of God in Christ.

After Azusa, entirely new denominations were formed on an explicitly Pentecostal basis. The Assemblies of God was founded in 1914 and attracted Christians with a Baptist background sympathetic to Durham's Finished Work teaching; it is now the largest Pentecostal denomination in the world, with about 67 million members. Later denominations were Elim Pentecostal Church (1915), the Pentecostal Church of God (1919), the International Church of the Foursquare Gospel (1927), and the Open Bible Standard Churches (1935). One of Classical Pentecostalism's most successful tools of outreach was not a church at all but the Full Gospel Business Men's Fellowship International, founded in 1952.

Acceptance of the "initial evidence" teaching is fairly common in Classical Pentecostal churches, especially those from North America. But this may mislead us into thinking that Classical Pentecostalism is chiefly concerned with the Holy Spirit and pays very little attention to the Son of God. By contrast, from the very beginning, Christ was at the center of Pentecostal belief. As summarized in the "Foursquare Gospel" of preacher Aimee Semple McPherson: Jesus is savior (John 3:16), baptizer in the Spirit (Acts 2:4), healer (Jas 5:14–15), and soon-coming king (I Thess 4:16–17). Belief in Christ starts with his saving work and extends to his promised return in glory. In between, he sends the Spirit upon his disciples and heals them. Pentecostals with a Holiness background will add that Jesus is also the sanctifier.

Take note: Pentecostals are *not* Fundamentalists. In fact, nobody despised, ostracized, and persecuted early Pentecostals more fiercely than Fundamentalists. Fundamentalism requires a literalistic approach to the Scripture that squeezes too tightly for Pentecostals to breathe. It also decisively rejects all manifestations of spiritual gifts after the close of the apostolic age. It is true that Pentecostals by and large take the Scripture with utter seriousness, but they don't take it the same way that Fundamentalists do. Inerrancy was not originally a Pentecostal concern, for example.

American Classical Pentecostals formed a fellowship body in 1948 called the Pentecostal Fellowship of North America. It recognized officially what had already long been happening unofficially: a great fluidity among Pentecostal denominations, along the lines of what Lutherans would call altar-and-pulpit fellowship. Its major flaw was that no African-American churches belonged to it. Finally recognizing this evil for what it was, the Fellowship disbanded in 1994 and a new group was established in its place, this time putting whites and blacks on equal footing: the Pentecostal/Charismatic Churches of North America. The event at which this racial reconciliation took place has been nicknamed the "Memphis Miracle" since it happened in Memphis, Tennessee. Full racial integration remains a challenge for Pentecostals—as it does for all other Christians on the planet.

In the year 2010 there were at least 89 million Christians belonging to Classical Pentecostal denominations around the world.[1]

Classical Oneness Pentecostals. As mentioned in the last chapter, in 1913 a new belief arose among certain Pentecostals claiming that Christians were to baptize in Jesus' name only, as in the Book of Acts, not in the name of the Father, Son, and Holy Spirit, as in Matthew 28:19 (which had been standard practice for virtually all of church history). In time, this led to the belief that all of the Godhead is present in Jesus. "Father," "Son," and "Spirit" are names for different manifestations or modes of Jesus. In essence, "Father, Son, and Holy Spirit" is just another way of saying "Jesus Christ." That in turn meant a denial of the Trinity, specifically the idea that God is eternally three Persons.

This anti-trinitarianism is quite different from previous Unitarian teachings that have arisen periodically in Christian history, since those had always denied the divinity of the Son and the Spirit, reserving it for the Father alone. Oneness teaching more closely resembles modalism, an early church heresy that taught that God wore different "masks" depending on how He dealt with people—sometimes as Father, sometimes as Son, sometimes as Spirit. This would mean that the three Persons are not truly God's own being but disguises or temporary appearances. Trinitarian Christianity by contrast confesses that the three Persons of Father, Son, and Holy Spirit *are* the one God, both in time and in eternity.

A further development of the Oneness movement (also called the Jesus' Name movement) was to compress salvation, sanctification, and Spirit baptism into one mega-experience. Baptism in the Spirit was not subsequent to salvation, as all other Classical Pentecostal churches have taught, but simultaneous to and equivalent with it.

Oneness denominations stemming from the early twentieth century include the United Pentecostal Church and the Pentecostal Assemblies of the World. They have tended to have greatest success in places were Islam is strong—perhaps because it is easier for Muslim converts to make the shift from the strict monotheism of Islam to the incarnation in Christianity this way—or in places where persecution by historic trinitarian churches has been sharpest, as in Mexico. A significant number of early African-American

1. It is notoriously difficult to get accurate statistics on the membership or reach of Pentecostal churches. This chapter follows the calculations of Johnson, "Counting Pentecostals Worldwide," 265–88.

Pentecostals also turned to the Oneness teaching, though it seems to have been caused as much by white Pentecostals' failure to accept and welcome black Christians as by doctrinal conviction.

Today there are about 2.7 million Oneness Pentecostals of the Classical type. It is clear that their teaching and practice deviate considerably more dramatically from historic Christian and Lutheran teaching than that of trinitarian Pentecostals. For this reason, in the rest of this book, we will assume that the Pentecostals of whom we speak are trinitarians who baptize in the name of the Father, Son, and Holy Spirit and who distinguish salvation from the experience of Spirit baptism. Oneness Pentecostals will always be identified as such.

However, it should be noted that in recent years trinitarian Pentecostals have striven toward better mutual understanding with Oneness Pentecostals. After many years of exclusion, Oneness adherents were admitted to the Society for Pentecostal Studies in 1973, and a lengthy dialogue was recently conducted between the two parties. Oneness churches see themselves and are seen by trinitarian Pentecostals as part of the Christian and Pentecostal family.

Charismatics. Classical Pentecostalism grew tremendously in the United States in its first two decades and then seemed to stall out. A fresh wave of revivals broke out in the late 1940s, in what was called the Latter Rain movement, but then again things went dormant. However, by this time, Pentecostals were no longer so virulently denounced by either Evangelical or mainline Protestants in America. Pentecostals were invited to be founding members of the National Association of Evangelicals in 1942, which further contributed to their respectability, at least in the United States. But the real surge in the legitimation of Pentecostal ideas and practice was the outbreak of the Charismatic movement in the "historic" churches.

Though there were foreshadowings of the Charismatic movement, just as there had been of the Azusa Street movement, the starting point for Charismatic renewal is generally attributed to an Episcopal priest in California, Dennis Bennett (1917–1991), who in the autumn of 1959 announced to his congregation that he had received the baptism in the Holy Spirit and the gift of tongues. A revival quickly broke out at his congregation and—with the legitimation that could only come from Pentecostal phenomena arising in such a staid and respectable environment as Episcopalianism—it spread to other Protestant mainline denominations as well.

Its most important impetus, though, came from its reception in the Catholic church. In 1967 Charismatic renewal took hold at two Catholic colleges (notably, among intellectuals) and found many champions in priests, bishops, and even Cardinal Léon Suenens of Belgium. By 2010 there were about 177 million Charismatic Catholics, and quite often they comprise the most vibrant elements of that church, especially in the state or folk church settings of Europe. Altogether there are roughly 235 million Charismatics distributed throughout the Catholic, Anglican, Protestant, and Orthodox churches.

We will turn to the question of Charismatic renewal in the Lutheran church in the next chapter.

Neocharismatics, also known as Neopentecostals, Independent Charismatics, Postdenominationalists, Restorationists, Radicals, Neo-Apostolics, and Third Wave Pentecostals. The fact that so many terms can be applied to this group is an indication of how general and rather unhelpful the terms are. Basically, the referent is a Christian church that exhibits typical Pentecostal/Charismatic practices but has no connection with Classical Pentecostal or mainline Charismatic churches. In short, they're start-ups. They usually have little awareness or interest in past Christian history, do not regard historic churches as legitimate (if they're even aware of their existence), and frown upon denominationalism. They can be anything from entirely independent congregations to networked affiliations of pastors and congregations. And there are far more of them than all the other types of Pentecostals put together. By the year 2010 it was estimated that there were about 258 million Neocharismatics, and the numbers have only continued to climb steeply upward ever since. The best estimates indicate that there are another 12 million Neocharismatics who have adopted the Oneness teaching.

Theologically, Neocharismatics are more likely to view conversion and Spirit baptism as a single experience, as do Oneness Pentecostals, but without drawing Oneness conclusions about the Trinity. Neocharismatics emphasize tongues less but healing, dreams, visions, and signs and wonders more. They are more likely to invent their own terminology and theologies than to use traditional Pentecostal or Charismatic versions.

Where do Neocharismatics come from? Many of them were forced out of or opted to leave their churches of origin, especially when those churches would not recognize the validity of their charismatic experiences. Others simply started up as independent ventures by leaders who experienced a call into ministry. Still others broke away from mission churches. In this respect, Neocharismatics are a variation on the theme of Nondenominationalism.

It is nearly impossible to summarize or generalize about this group, other than to note their emphasis on the experienced power and gifts of the Holy Spirit and an intense missionary passion. Still, it will be helpful to look at some significant subsets within the Neocharismatic family.

African-Initiated Churches. The AICs (also called African Independent Churches or African-Instituted Churches) have their origins in the late nineteenth and early twentieth century. They have been defined as "founded in Africa, by Africans, and primarily for Africans."[2] They evolved largely as a result of two factors: 1) frustration at the limitations imposed upon African Christians by European and North American mission leaders, who often would not ordain indigenous believers or tolerate worship practices that arose from African culture; and 2) the translation of the Bible into indigenous African languages, which ironically enough usually came about through the work of those same missionaries. Reading the Bible for themselves, Africans found firm ground on which to question the missionaries' practice—everything from the style of worship to structures of leadership to manifestations of the Spirit. The AICs sought to express Christian belief in ways that made sense to their own worldview and lived experience, and in so doing issued a sharp critique to the rationalistic approach taken by Christian believers from the North. Rather than being book- and analysis-oriented, they tend to be oral- and narrative-oriented. On the whole, healing is the most central and pervasive concern of such churches. Here again we see the link between Pentecostal practice and an increased attunement to cultural indigenization.

Chinese house churches. China today has more Christians engaging in Pentecostal practices than any other country in the world except Brazil and the United States. From 1975 to 1990, after the death of Mao Tse-Tung and a decline in the persecution of believers, the number of Christians in China grew from 1.5 million to 78 million, of which 65 percent are Neocharismatics. The greatest growth has been seen in the House Church Movement, which had already started to grow well before 1990. House churches, or private circles of believers, allowed the development of Christian faith among people who would have been endangered if their faith had been publicly demonstrated. Pentecostal practice was well-suited to the house

2. Anderson, *African Reformation*, 10, quoting Harold Turner.

churches, since by the limitations imposed upon them a formal liturgical or clerical structure would have made little sense. House churches thrived on being informal and spontaneous. A personal experience of the Holy Spirit secured the loyalty and gave the strength needed to stay Christian in such a hostile environment. Here, too, healing has been a major emphasis. The theology of such informal churches ranges from highly orthodox to extremely marginal.

Latin American grassroots churches. It is by now a well-known fact that although Latin America has traditionally been Roman Catholic, Pentecostal churches of all types have made significant inroads. (And those who remain Roman Catholic are often highly charismatic.) It is not always clear where the boundary line is, as many people move from one church to another without officially withdrawing or joining. In general, Latin Americans looking for an alternative to Catholicism—whether for spiritual, cultural, or political reasons—turn to the exuberant and media-savvy Neocharismatic churches. These have also tended to attract the poor and people of color through their strong emphasis on prosperity and moral discipline, which has led to increased social mobility. Among the largest Neocharismatic churches are those of Brazil: Brasil para Cristo, Deus é Amor, and the Igreja Universal do Reino do Deus, the last of which has 12 million members and intense evangelism campaigns in Europe and North America.

American Nondenominational churches. Independent churches with Pentecostal features started to appear in the U.S. in the 1970s, but they really began to boom in the 1990s. While continuing the habit of warm, emotional worship, they imposed fewer restrictions on members' behavior than the Classical Pentecostal churches did. Many such Neocharismatic churches were founded by people on the fringe of the Classical Pentecostal or Charismatic movements who wished to be free of wider ecclesiastical control. Nevertheless, despite the trend toward the total independence of each local congregation (a polity that had been embraced by Baptists centuries before), many such churches and pastors are connected to one another through fellowships or networks, some of which establish criteria and offer credentials for ordination. Examples of such networked Neocharismatic churches in the U.S. are Calvary Chapel, Hope Chapel, and the Association of Vineyard Churches, which has exercised its greatest influence through its widely admired contemporary Christian music. Key figures are Peter Wagner and John Wimber with their emphasis on "power encounters" through signs and wonders.

It is worth noting that there has been a recent trend in scholarship to get away from dissecting terms like "Classical Pentecostal," "Charismatic," and so forth, and instead to name the whole complex of these Christian phenomena as "the Renewal." In this respect, the term "the Renewal" functions as an all-encompassing description analogous to the use of "the Reformation" to describe Lutheran, Calvinist, Zwinglian, Anglican, Anabaptist, Spiritualist, and Roman Catholic movements in the sixteenth century. If we look at the Renewal as one single if multi-faceted event stretching over more than a century, then its adherents today number somewhere around 600 million. But to make the terminology a bit simpler here, we will stick with the term "Pentecostal" to refer to the whole spectrum of the Renewal. We will use additional terms like Classical or Neocharismatic when it's especially important to distinguish among the types.

For Further Reading

David D. Barrett, "The 20th Century Pentecostal/Charismatic Renewal of the Holy Spirit, with its Goal of World Evangelization," *International Bulletin of Missionary Research* 2/3 (1988) 119–29 was the pioneer study to propose a taxonomy of renewal movements into Classical Pentecostal, Charismatic, and Independent Charismatic. Barrett proposes terming all the movements collectively as Renewalist.

The Pew Forum recently released a study on the distribution of Christians globally and denominationally: "Global Christianity—A Report on the Size and Distribution of the World's Christian Population," available online at <www.pewforum.org/2011/12/19/global-christianity-exec/>.

The dialogue statement "Oneness-Trinitarian Pentecostal Final Report, 2002–2007," along with papers by the dialogue team members, can be found in the journal *Pneuma* 30/2 (2008) 203–24.

The most detailed study of AICs is to be found in Allan Anderson, *African Reformation: African Initiated Christianity in the 21st Century* (Trenton: Africa World, 2001).

A recent look at the Chinese house church phenomenon based on firsthand interviews can be found in Eugene Bach and Brother Zhu, *Crimson Cross: Uncovering the Mysteries of the Chinese House Church* (Blountsville: Fifth Estate, 2012).

CHAPTER 3

Lutherans

WHY HAVE A CHAPTER *about* Lutherans in a book about Pentecostals *for* Lutherans?

In ecumenical encounters, what you have always taken for granted suddenly becomes the focus of attention for the first time. It stops being the background or foundation of reality and starts being perceived as one possible choice among many. So it is here as well. For Lutherans to read about Pentecostalism and talk with Pentecostals is to think differently about Lutheranism, to see it in a new light. This chapter, therefore, offers a very brief overview of Lutheran history for those who wish for a deeper understanding of their own past, precisely in the context of conversation with other Christians. Hopefully it will inspire readers to dig deeper into the details of their own Lutheran history!

What makes a Lutheran church *Lutheran*? It is not a matter of location or culture. There are Lutherans in Australia, Bolivia, Canada, Romania, Singapore, and Tanzania—and many more countries besides. Some churches are quite old, dating back to the first millennium and having adopted the Reformation in the sixteenth century. Some are extremely new, the product of immigration, missions, and local adaptation.

Another matter of variety is church polity. Lutherans will have anything from an almost-congregational to an episcopal form of church government, and in different places they will place greater or lesser emphasis on the importance of that particular ecclesiastical structure. Some are widely connected with other churches in their own country as well as with churches abroad; some are relatively isolated.

There is also variety in worship. Some Lutheran churches conduct a liturgy quite like Luther's revision of the historic mass, while others have a more informal style.

The point is this: you can't assess what makes a Lutheran church *Lutheran* based on your own everyday experience of a Lutheran church. You may go elsewhere and find that the local Lutheran congregation resembles your own—but it may not. For that matter, you may go to a non-Lutheran congregation in another place and find that it is quite like your own church, more so than the Lutherans there! Some Christian churches are indeed distinguished from others by their *structure* and/or by their *liturgy*—the Roman Catholic, Eastern Orthodox, and Oriental Orthodox churches are examples of this, and to a lesser extent so is Anglicanism—but Lutheranism is not.

What, then, makes a Lutheran church Lutheran?

The answer is: a Lutheran church is a *confessional* church. That means it is defined and distinguished from other churches primarily by its beliefs, rather than by its structure or order of worship.

During the breakdown in negotiations between Luther's evangelical followers and the authorities loyal to the pope in 1530, the Lutherans were given an opportunity to present their views at the Diet of Augsburg, convened by Emperor Charles V. Luther had to remain hidden at the Coburg Castle some distance away from Augsburg because he was under the imperial ban, so it fell to his Wittenberg colleague, Philip Melanchthon, to draw up a statement of faith. This document came to be known as the Augsburg Confession. Out of a total of twenty-eight articles, the first twenty-one emphasized the common faith gladly inherited from the medieval and ancient church and still held in common with the Roman party: God, original sin, the Son of God, justification by faith, the office of preaching, the new obedience, the church, what the church is, baptism, the Lord's Supper, confession, repentance, the use of the sacraments, church order, church traditions, civil affairs, Christ's return in judgment, free will, the cause of sin, good works, and the place of the saints in Christian piety. The last seven articles detailed the correction of abuses, explaining why Lutherans offered the Lord's Supper to the laypeople in both kinds, allowed priests to marry, eliminated the part of the communion liturgy that suggests that Christ is being sacrificed, made private confession a matter of choice rather than a requirement, no longer imposed fasting regulations, no longer held people to monastic vows, and denied the right of church authorities to exercise political power.

The Augsburg Confession, although written in a situation of trial and self-defense, so beautifully captured what the new evangelical movement believed that it became the rallying point and ultimately the "charter document" for Lutheran churches. It has been adopted by all subsequent Lutheran churches, including those that were established long after the sixteenth century ended. It has always gone hand in hand with the Small Catechism, a summary of the basic points of the Christian faith published by Luther in 1529 for use in the family, which later became the chief text used in confirmation instruction for young people. Member churches of the Lutheran World Federation subscribe to both the Augsburg Confession and the Small Catechism.

A large number of Lutheran churches further subscribe to all the contents of the Book of Concord, sometimes referred to as the Concordia or the Lutheran Confessions. (Even those churches that don't formally subscribe to it regard the documents in it as important and worthy.) The Book of Concord was assembled in 1580 after many years of trying to iron out the conflicts within the nascent Lutheran movement—to say nothing of the ongoing political intrigue with Roman Catholics and among the various kinds of Protestants. The book starts with the three ancient Creeds: the Apostles', the Nicene, and the Athanasian. From Luther's era, it includes the Augsburg Confession, the Apology of the Augsburg Confession (which Melanchthon had written in 1531 to clear up misunderstandings in the Roman Confutation), the Smalcald Articles (written by Luther in 1537 in preparation for a possible church council and as a kind of theological last will and testament, since he thought he would die soon, though in fact he didn't die until 1546), the Treatise on the Power and Primacy of the Pope (written by Philip Melanchthon on the same occasion as the Smalcald Articles), and Luther's Small and Large Catechisms (the latter intended for pastors). Finally, the Book of Concord includes the Formula of Concord, a kind of doctrinal peace treaty composed in 1577 and signed by most Lutheran pastors in Germany at that time, which exists in shorter form as the Epitome and in longer form as the Solid Declaration.

The Confessional documents were never meant to be a substitute for the holy Scriptures. They were not even meant as a substitute for the Creeds. Both Bible and Creed rate higher, in Lutheran estimation, than specifically Lutheran documents. But from the beginning, Lutherans recognized the need to walk a fine line between holding to the Scripture as the only true source and norm of Christian faith, and dealing with the inevitable misunderstandings and distortions of the Christian faith that arise from misuse of the biblical text. After all, even the devil can quote Scripture (Matt 4:6). The

Confessions were meant to be a guide to the right reading and understanding of the Scripture and the Creeds.

For, as Luther once put it, how are we to know what the word of God is, when there are so many words of God? His answer: Jesus Christ is the Word of God. All the words of God in Scripture point toward him. He is the key for understanding all the different books, genres, and details found in our widely varied holy Scriptures. The purpose of the Lutheran Confessions is to put Christ at the center of Christian faith and to receive him as the key to understanding the whole.

The Confessions were not meant to be exhaustive. They don't (and don't presume to) answer every question that might come up in the life of the church or to impose artificial limits on what counts as theology. For instance, the Confessions don't have mission to new lands on their horizon, so they offer no advice about how to go about it. Rather, the Confessions are regulative in the sense of always pointing our theology back to the Creeds, to the scriptural canon, and above all to Jesus Christ, giving us direction that can be adapted to our current situations. In this respect, the Confessions direct mission (for example) insofar as they testify that Christ is the center of our proclamation, allow for variety in worship practice, and commend the importance of the vernacular.

It should finally be mentioned that, although only a few of Luther's writings have Confessional status, they have been an ongoing source of inspiration, instruction, direction, and correction for Lutheran churches. About half of Luther's extant writings are biblical commentaries. Beyond those are sermons, devotional guides, letters to friends and people in need, treatises written for specific occasions, and disputations for use in the university setting. The "Luther Renaissance" in the twentieth century saw to the re-publication of most of his writings—many of which had been lost or forgotten over the centuries—and gave a burst of new life to the study of his works. Among the most important of Luther's writings are The Sermon on Two Kinds of Righteousness, The Freedom of a Christian, The Babylonian Captivity of the Church, The Address to the Christian Nobility, Confession Concerning Christ's Supper, Concerning Rebaptism, The Bondage of the Will, the Commentary on Galatians, and On the Councils and the Church. His hymns have also deeply shaped Lutheran piety over the years, above all "A Mighty Fortress Is Our God."

This is, of course, why Lutheran churches are called "Lutheran." The term was originally a derogatory one to denounce those who shared Luther's concerns for the reform of the church, though his allies proudly accepted the label. Luther's own word for his movement was "evangelical," meaning "of the gospel," from the Greek word for gospel, *euangelion*. Nowadays "evangelical" has taken on other meanings. In German, *evangelisch* means "Protestant" generally. In American English, "evangelical" most often refers to the heirs of Reformed and Methodist revivals in early American history. However, the importance of the word hangs on in the fact that most Lutheran churches use both terms to describe themselves: the Evangelical Lutheran Church of Costa Rica, the Japan Evangelical Lutheran Church. Some specify what kind of "evangelical" they are by referring back to the Lutheran Confessions, as in the Evangelical Church of the Augsburg Confession in the Slovak Republic.

Not much has been said so far of *what* exactly Lutherans believe via these Confessions, other than the centrality of Christ; we'll take that up in future chapters as we work through Pentecostal beliefs and practices. But before continuing we should recognize that Lutheranism did not remain static in the centuries following the Book of Concord. Another 450 years have built upon the foundation laid by Luther and his friends. Lutheran churches have seen a variety of ups and downs, movements and trends, fallings away and regroupings. A constant danger when we speak of ourselves is to speak only of the ideal version of ourselves, of ourselves on paper. But we—and others—encounter the real, lived, historical version of ourselves. How others react to us depends on what they actually find, not on what we think they should find, and vice versa. So it will help to know a little bit about where the Lutheran story has gone since the sixteenth century. In so doing, we will see where it begins to intersect with the story of Pentecostal movements.

Although Lutherans denied the conflation of the bishop's office with that of the prince, the reality is that very early on they found themselves dependent upon secular powers to protect and advance their cause. The ultimate fate of the Lutheran movement swung back and forth a number of times until finally it became clear that the Roman forces could not stamp it out through sheer military effort. Nevertheless, at that time, nobody thought it was possible for different faiths to coexist in the same political unit (the uneasy position of the Jews is sad evidence of this). Therefore, the compromise that the two sides worked out was one of *cuius regio, eius religio*: whoever the region, his the religion. The prince chose to be Roman

Catholic or Lutheran and then expected all his people to follow suit. If they didn't like it, they could emigrate to another territory. Many did just that.

In the meantime, the Lutheran movement spread outside of Luther's Saxony. In addition to the various regional Lutheran churches that arose in Germany, the Reformation was adopted by all the Nordic countries: today's Iceland, Norway, Denmark, Sweden, and Finland, sometimes with a minimum of disruption in the process. Lutheranism also took hold in the Baltic region, especially in today's Latvia and Estonia. It was warmly received in eastern Europe, especially in Slovakia and Hungary, but a rather brutal Counter-Reformation on the part of the Catholics almost entirely reversed this process, leaving behind only the small Lutheran churches that have survived to this day. The religious tensions never fully quieted down, exploding in the most appalling bloodshed Europe had ever seen, the Thirty Years' War (1618–1648). Certainly politics and imperialism were mixed up with religious motivations, and at times Protestants and Catholics of one region would join forces against Protestants and Catholics of another. But the staggering cruelty of this three-decade-long war dealt an almost mortal blow to the credibility of the Christian faith in Europe, a legacy that continues to the present.

We should take note of one trend in particular here. A major emphasis of the Reformation was the importance of having worship and the Scripture in the vernacular, the local language. Everywhere the Reformation spread, Latin was abandoned as the liturgical language and Bible translation projects got underway. Furthermore, Lutherans had come to distrust the universal and centralizing oversight epitomized in the papacy. Thus, each region, kingdom, or language group was entitled to its own church and its own government. Although Lutherans in different countries remained connected to one another in various ways, especially by pastoral candidates who traveled to study at the various universities with Lutheran faculties, there was no longer any necessary or structural relationship between them. Each was free to go its own way and develop its own particular emphases. The strength and weakness of such a system is immediately evident. On the one hand, it allows for a new measure of cultural adaptation of the gospel and decision-making on the part of those most affected and best able to understand the local situation. On the other hand, it easily leads to a parochial and individualistic outlook manipulated by local considerations and politics.

Despite the rejection of papal oversight, Lutherans—like almost all Christians at that time—assumed a tight connection between church and state. In many places, the Lutheran church became the state church or the folk church. It was privileged and endorsed by the government; the royalty were required to be members of that church; clergy were financially supported by the state; the state often had some say in the election of bishops or superintendents; the state gradually took upon itself the diaconal work of the church; and so on. In some places, the sheer fact of being born in a nation made one automatically a member of the state church, quite apart from baptism! The church could influence government and society to a great degree, but the government and society could also influence the church to a great degree.

Within the European Lutheran churches, two trends developed, partly in response to the new legal situation and partly in response to ongoing conflict with other Christians. One is what came to be called Lutheran Orthodoxy. Its emphasis was on the mind, on right understanding—a natural outgrowth of the university origins of the Reformation. Especially as shots were fired (literally and figuratively) between Lutherans, Roman Catholics, and the Reformed, the goal of Lutheran Orthodoxy was to articulate as precisely and comprehensively as possible the beliefs of the Lutheran church and the errors of others' theology. At the same time, Lutheran Orthodox theologians composed many devotional works intended to assist laypeople in the cultivation of their piety. The other trend was Pietism. While the "grandfather of Pietism," Johann Arndt (1555–1621), was of tough intellectual fiber himself, he lamented the loss of the heart in Lutheran churches. Noting Luther's concern for love, joy, and transformation in response to the gospel, in addition to the right understanding of it, Arndt's book *True Christianity* commended the path of personal regeneration. His concerns were picked up a generation later by Philipp Spener (1635–1705) in the *Pia Desideria* ("Pious Desires").

In reality a human being has both a head and a heart, but in the history of Lutheranism a chasm began to develop between the two. This had implications for relationships with other Christians as well. The Lutheran Orthodox, keenly aware of Lutheran distinctives, were hostile toward closer bonds with the Reformed, while Pietists tended to judge everyone who'd experienced "the new birth" or displayed a lively faith as a true brother or sister in Christ, regardless of what they thought. The Lutheran Orthodox maintained the importance of the church's public role in society, while the Pietists tended to withdraw from political leadership, preferring to invest their energies in economic development and missions instead. Pietists also showed a marked distrust toward the official state or folk church, preferring the company of an *ecclesiola in ecclesia*, a "little church in the church." These are broad strokes, of course, but there is enough truth in them to have created a lasting distrust between different kinds of Lutherans as a result. Pietism continued to be a distinct movement well into the twentieth century. Lutheran Orthodoxy was gradually succeeded by the university form of theological study and evolved into the nineteenth century's "scientific" approach to theology and the Scripture. The origins of the modern historical-critical study of the Bible lie in German Lutheran theology faculties.

In the eighteenth century, two new things happened that radically changed the face of Lutheranism: immigration and missions.

Immigration out of Europe, primarily to North America but also to South America and Australia, began in the 1700s in response to ongoing violence and especially economic pressures. People left seeking a better life for themselves. Some made a point of taking their faith with them. Others, who had been nominally associated with their state or folk church, more or less forgot it when they arrived on new shores. The churches back home soon recognized the spiritual desert awaiting their émigrés and began sending clergy to round them up and organize them into new churches. Many of these started out as extensions of the European church but, either by their own efforts or by the changing political fortunes of their new homeland, they became independent. The bonds to the home church were Confessional and, at least for awhile, linguistic, but no longer structural.

Mission, meanwhile, finally became a feature of Lutheranism around this same time. The reformers had believed that the era of mission was already over: the Great Commission had been addressed to the apostles but did not carry over to the present day. (This despite the late arrival of Christianity in many parts of Europe, a thousand years or more after the resurrection.) Some Lutherans went so far as to call mission a Catholic heresy! This may have been connected to a critique of the imperial expansion of Spain, for instance, into Central and South America. On the other hand, many Lutheran churches only began their missions once their own nations got involved in the imperial race. Despite the mixed fortunes of such efforts, many Lutheran missionaries took a strong stand against Western abuses of indigenous peoples, opened schools and codified the local language, defended the poor and offered medical service to the sick, and of course shared the gospel of Jesus Christ. In India, for instance,

Lutheran Christianity dates back to the arrival in 1706 of the missionary Bartholomäus Ziegenbalg (1682–1719) in today's state of Tamil Nadu. Here also, in the case of mission, the new Lutheran churches were neither state nor folk churches—certainly never majority churches—but independent structures in varying kinds of relationship to the state. As is the case everywhere, mission churches really began to grow when the local people made it their own and became the chief agents of evangelism instead of only its recipients.

As we have already seen, the Pentecostal movement arose in the early twentieth century and got a big burst of energy from the Azusa Street revival, which had its own roots in the Holiness and Methodist movements. It's worth noting, then, that one of the streams that fed into Holiness and Methodist Christianity was Lutheran Pietism. John Wesley, in fact, had his famous conversion experience on account of his heart being "strangely warmed" while reading Luther's Preface to Romans about justification by faith alone and the righteousness that comes as a sheer gift of God. Wesley had connections with Lutheran Pietists on the European continent, among them Johann Albrecht Bengel (1687–1752), many of whom put a great stress on holy living. Divine healing was also a marked feature of Pietism, especially in the ministry of Johann Christoph Blumhardt (1805–1880) and his son, who practiced exorcism on occasion. Other areas of Europe had also seen proto-Pentecostal movements among Lutherans, in particular in two revivals that raced through Finland, the Awakened movement under the leadership of Paavo Ruotsalainen (1777–1852) in the late eighteenth and early nineteenth centuries, and the Laestadian movement named for Lars Levi Laestadius (1800–1861) later in the nineteenth century. Both of these were characterized by spiritual phenomena of various kinds and were not especially well received by official church structures.

It was, however, the Pentecostal movement itself that led to the most virulent condemnation. There is, for example, the case of Jonathan Paul (1853–1931), a German Pietist pastor who belonged to a renewal group called the Gnadauer Verband. In 1907 he visited Oslo, and while there he received the "baptism in the Spirit" experience and spoke in tongues. He brought the Pentecostal movement home with him. However, within two years, fifty-six pastors within the Verband authored the *Berliner Erklärung* ("Berlin Declaration") identifying the Pentecostal experience with the work of the devil. Paul and others responded with the Mühlheim Declaration, attempting to refute the charges, but the damage was done. Paul left the state church to join a new Pentecostal denomination, the *Mülheimer Verband freikirchlich evangelischer Gemeinden* (which, perhaps not surprisingly, is quite Lutheran in its theology, as Pentecostal churches go). The divorce was long-lasting, but in 1995 German Pietists and Pentecostal/Charismatics came together to sign a *Bussbekenntnis versöhnungswilliger Christen*—"a confession of repentance by Christians who are open to reconciliation"— declaring the 1909 Berlin Declaration null and void.

The previous chapter noted the eruption of the Charismatic movement within the historic churches. The Lutheran churches were no exception. In the early 1960s the charismata were experienced among American Lutherans, and the pattern quickly followed in Europe. The response of the official churches varied. The American Lutheran Church (a predecessor of today's Evangelical Lutheran Church in America), for instance, sent a team of theologians along with a psychologist to investigate the phenomena, assuming the participants in the revival to be mentally unstable or easily manipulable. They were quite startled to discover how normal everyone was! None of the Lutheran churches took extreme measures to stamp out charismatic phenomena, choosing mainly to ignore them instead, but in some cases there were indeed active attempts to separate Charismatic pastors from Charismatic congregations. In other cases, the official church released a statement identifying the acceptable theological parameters of Charismatic practice, some more positively disposed and some more negative.

The most important Charismatic renewal among Lutherans, however, has taken place in eastern Africa. In 1970s Ethiopia, Lutheran youth came in contact with Pentecostals, began experiencing the charismata, and almost immediately came into conflict with congregational authorities. Under the guidance of the Mekane Yesus church's General Secretary, Gudina Tumsa (1929–1979, later a martyr under the Derg regime), a team of forty met to compose a statement on the Charismatic renewal. It was interpreted as the long hoped-for and prayed-for revival to empower their mission. In this way, Charismatic practice was positively received and integrated within the structure of Lutheran thought. A similar process took place in Tanzania, where Charismatic practice was the inheritance of the earlier twentieth-century *Uamsho* revival across eastern Africa. This process of adaptation happened in every historic church with a Charismatic revival, whether Protestant or Catholic. Instead of accepting as finished products the conclusions of Classical Pentecostalism, Charismatic theologians set out to reinterpret the phenomena and their consequences in the light of their received theology. Today, the Charismatic Lutheran churches of Africa are the fastest-growing Lutheran churches in the world and seem likely soon to be the largest as well (the Mekane Yesus church went from 200,000 members in 1980 to well over 7 million in 2015).

Other Lutheran churches have had a more difficult experience with both Charismatics and Neocharismatics. For instance, in Brazil there has been a tendency among Charismatics, even within the Lutheran church, to deny the validity and efficacy of infant baptism. Regardless of region, many Lutherans perceive all kinds of Pentecostalism as a fundamental threat to their own people and teaching, as Lutherans are either lured away by "sheep stealers" or voluntarily leave as they are attracted to Pentecostal communities.

As we now finally approach a more detailed exploration of Pentecostalism from a Lutheran perspective, we need to draw two conclusions from the foregoing.

The first is that, while Lutheranism is a *confessional* movement, Pentecostalism is an *experiential* movement. Lutherans often have trouble getting a handle on what exactly Pentecostals do and believe, precisely because their self-understanding as Christians has not developed in a way parallel to that of Lutherans. Pentecostals will exhibit what seem to Lutherans to be a bewildering array of beliefs, with no codified results or any way to adjudicate between them (despite acknowledging some basic foundations like the Holy Trinity or salvation as a gift from God). Pressing Pentecostals on typical Lutheran questions—such as, how do you understand the relationship between faith and works? what do you think of the two kingdoms or the three estates? what is the nature of Christ's presence in the Lord's Supper?—will produce answers more or less acceptable. But it won't help Lutherans see what makes Pentecostals *Pentecostal*. The common feature across all the many types of Pentecostalism is the *experience* of the Holy Spirit in the Christian's life and the resulting exercise of spiritual gifts like tongues, healing, and prophecy.

The second point is this: because Pentecostalism is neither confessional, nor liturgical, nor structural, but experiential, it crosses boundaries easily. In this respect, it resembles the Lutheran experience with Pietism the most. The Pentecostal experience can coexist with Catholic structure (at least 11 percent of Catholics are Charismatics); with Anglican liturgy (the Charismatic movement in America began with an Episcopal priest);

and with the Lutheran Confessions (as the assorted Lutheran Charismatics in the world have shown). Many Pentecostals have drawn their own firm conclusions about what church structure or liturgy or doctrine should look like as a result of their experience of the Spirit. But because Pentecostals are characterized by an experience, their borders cannot remain impermeable. And indeed, to this extent, what is distinctively, experientially Pentecostal already exists within Lutheranism.

Thus it is quite inaccurate to think and speak with a sharp "us vs. them" mentality. Such would be inappropriate anyway, since we are all Christians who worship the same Lord. But it is doubly so if we start with the assumption that Pentecostal experience is something other than and foreign to Lutheranism. The fact that they are already "within the walls" may make our relations with Pentecostals easier, or may make them harder, but either way it is not a fact that we can ignore.

Having established the foundation, it is time now to look more closely at Pentecostal churches, their beliefs and their practices, and how they intersect with both Confessional and Charismatic Lutheranism.

For Further Reading

The Book of Concord: The Confessions of the Evangelical Lutheran Church, eds. Robert Kolb and Timothy J. Wengert (Minneapolis: Fortress, 2000). Other translations of the Book of Concord can easily be found online in many languages.

Two good histories of Lutheranism are Eric W. Gritsch, *A History of Lutheranism*, 2nd ed. (Minneapolis: Fortress, 2010), and E. Clifford Nelson, *The Rise of World Lutheranism: An American Perspective* (Philadelphia: Fortress, 1982).

Presence, Power, Praise: Documents on the Charismatic Renewal, ed. Kilian McDonnell (Collegeville: Liturgical Press, 1980). This three-volume collection contains a number of official statements by Lutheran churches regarding Pentecostalism and Charismatic renewal, as well as statements by many other churches.

Regin Prenter, *Spiritus Creator* (Eugene: Wipf and Stock, 2001 [1953]), is an excellent study of Luther's doctrine of the Holy Spirit.

Carter Lindberg, *The Third Reformation? Charismatic Movements and the Lutheran Tradition* (Macon: Mercer University Press, 1983) and the abbreviated version *Charismatic Renewal and the Lutheran Tradition*, LWF Report No. 21 (Geneva: Lutheran World Federation, 1985) take a more critical approach to Charismatic renewal from a Lutheran theological perspective.

Victor C. Pfitzner, *Led by the Spirit: How Charismatic is New Testament Christianity?* (Adelaide: Open Book, 1976) and Larry Christenson, *Welcome, Holy Spirit: A Study of Charismatic Renewal in the Church* (Minneapolis: Augsburg, 1987) take a more positive approach to Charismatic renewal from a Lutheran theological perspective.

Consultation on Renewal Movements in Lutheran Churches in North and South, ed. Péri Rasolondraibe (Geneva: Lutheran World Federation, 2002) is a collection of papers offered by Lutherans coming mainly from Charismatic backgrounds.

CHAPTER 4

Baptism I

BAPTISM LIES AT THE crux of the difference and misunderstanding between Pentecostals and Lutherans. This is no great surprise, since the term "baptism" can refer to two entirely different things in our respective theological languages. Lutherans and Pentecostals both acknowledge and practice water baptism, though as a rule they interpret it in very different ways. Pentecostals, however, advocate a distinct "baptism in the Spirit," which they base on passages in Acts and believe to be a possibility for the church today. Charismatics, including the Lutherans among them, have generally endorsed a special experience of the Spirit, usually with some modifications to Pentecostal theory and terminology. But "Spirit baptism" was no part of the sixteenth-century conversation and thus is not dealt with in the Lutheran Confessions.

In contrast to our first several chapters describing Pentecostal and Lutheran origins and history, now in these next three chapters we turn to biblical exegesis and application. In this first of two chapters on baptism, we will work through the accounts of water baptism and the Holy Spirit in Luke-Acts. Certainly there is a great deal about baptism and the Spirit in the other New Testament books, too. But because Luke-Acts has functioned as a "canon within a canon" for Pentecostals (much like Romans and Galatians for Lutherans), we will restrict our discussion to these two books. Luke and Acts do, in any event, comprise about one-quarter of the New Testament, so if Lutherans claim to have a biblical theology, they will need to offer as clear an account of these two books as Pentecostals do!

The question we will pursue in this chapter is: are baptism in water and baptism in the Holy Spirit two separate things, or are they the same thing? As we work through the evidence, our goal will be primarily to understand what Acts is trying to tell us about baptism and the Spirit, apart from the specific confessional questions we put to it. The secondary goal will be to do justice to both Lutheran and Pentecostal interpretations of Acts and their experiences of baptism and the Spirit. There must be *some* good reason why both communities have derived their distinctive theologies from the Bible but have arrived at differing conclusions. In this way, both sets of Christians will be encouraged to strengthen their teaching and pastoral practice as well as to understand one another better. In the next chapter we'll turn to further interpretation and application of what we learn here. And in the chapter after that, we'll examine the biblical witness regarding charismata or spiritual gifts.

The seminal challenge in the interpretation of baptism lies in John the Baptist's prophecy in Luke 3:16 (cf. Mark 1:8, Matthew 3:11, John 1:33): "I baptize you with water, but he who is mightier than I is coming, the strap of whose sandals I am not worthy to untie. He will baptize you with the Holy Spirit and fire."

The first thing to recognize is that, in the biblical account, it is *John the Baptist* who starts the business of baptizing in water, not Jesus. According to John 3:22, Jesus baptizes some time after John the Baptist does, but then in John 4:2 a correction is made, stating that only Jesus' disciples baptized, not Jesus himself. Neither Jesus nor the disciples ever baptize in the Synoptic Gospels.

Why then does John the Baptist perform baptism, and what does it mean? In all four Gospels, John the Baptist's is what we might call a "testimonial baptism." To be baptized by John is to identify oneself with repentant Israel, with the true Israel that recognizes how far it has fallen from the Lord God's intentions. John's actions are understood by the Evangelists as the preparation for Jesus, who dies on the cross in order to save people from sin. Repentance is the appropriate way to welcome such a savior.

Jesus also receives this baptism, which often puzzles Lutherans. Since Jesus was not a sinner, why did he need to get baptized and so be forgiven? The confusion arises from retrojecting Christian baptism back onto John's baptism. Jesus receives John's baptism to identify himself and his ministry with repentant Israel, as we can see in Jesus' own preaching of repentance. The difference is that Jesus, as the Lord, also has the authority to forgive sins. John does not. John can only call people to repentance, but he himself cannot forgive them in his own name. He can invite people to the forgiveness of sins, but he cannot actually bestow it (Luke 3:3). Jesus is not forgiven by receiving John's baptism—no one is! By receiving John's baptism,

Jesus is instead identifying himself with a repentant Israel that hopes for the forgiveness of sins.

Right after Jesus' baptism by John, something unexpected happens: the Holy Spirit descends in the form of a dove and rests upon Jesus, and there is a declaration from heaven: "You are My beloved Son; with you I am well pleased." That is not what usually happened when John baptized! In this way Jesus' baptism foreshadows Christian baptism and its distinction from John's baptism, because in this one instance, uniquely, the Holy Spirit is involved. This event also inaugurates Jesus' ministry, sending him out to undertake his earthly work. Finally, Jesus' baptism foreshadows his destiny: going under the water signifies his crucifixion, coming up out of it again signifies his resurrection, and the descent of the Spirit signifies Pentecost and all of the apostolic ministry that will flow from it.

So already in Luke 3 we find a critical distinction being made between *John's water baptism* and *Christian water baptism*. This distinction is a central concern of the Book of Acts and absolutely crucial to its understanding of both baptism and the Holy Spirit. Lutheran confusion about the baptism of the sinless Jesus originates in the failure to distinguish between the two kinds of baptism. The Pentecostal case for Spirit baptism suffers from the same failure to distinguish between them.

But in fact, in confusing these two water baptisms, contemporary Christians are making the same mistake that the early Christians made, which Luke-Acts took such pains to correct. The reason for the confusion is simple: the two baptisms look so much alike! Both use water. Both are connected to the repentance and forgiveness of sins. Both identify the baptized with the true Israel. It's not at all surprising that some people would fail to distinguish the one from the other. But in Acts, as we will see, two new elements are added to John's baptism to make it a new, Christian baptism: 1) the gift of the Holy Spirit and 2) the extension of the people of God beyond the borders of Israel to include all the nations of the earth.

At the end of Luke's Gospel, Jesus charges his disciples to proclaim "repentance and forgiveness of sins in his name to all nations, beginning from Jerusalem" (24:47) but also to wait to receive "power from on high" (24:49). In Acts 1, just before his ascension, Jesus refers back to John the Baptist's prophecy: "John baptized with water, but you will be baptized with the Holy Spirit not many days from now" (1:5). He repeats his own words from Luke 24, "you will receive power when the Holy Spirit has come upon you," and adds the specific purpose for the power: "you will be my witnesses in Jerusalem and in all Judea and Samaria, and to the end of the earth" (1:8).

Notice that *two distinct promises* regarding the Spirit are being made. One is the promised baptism in the Spirit, in direct contrast to John's water-only baptism. The other is the empowerment by the Spirit for the sake of mission to the world, in contrast to John's repentance-only baptism.

In Acts 2, what Jesus has promised in Acts 1 takes place. The disciples "were all filled with the Holy Spirit" (2:4). This allowed them to speak in many foreign languages so that the Jews—*only* Jews at this point!—who were visiting Jerusalem from all over the world would be able to understand their preaching. This is the "power from on high" that kindles the mission, first of all in Jerusalem, as Jesus said. When Peter preaches, he cites the prophet Joel as evidence of God's age-old promise that His Spirit would be shed on all people, young and old, male and female. When the stricken crowds ask what they should do, Peter replies, "Repent and be baptized every one of you in the name of Jesus Christ for the forgiveness of your sins, and you will receive the gift of the Holy Spirit" (2:38).

Notice again the similarity to John's baptism. The baptism to which Peter invites them still uses *water*, still involves *repentance*, still is for the sake of *forgiveness*, and so far is addressed only to *Israel*. The tremendous difference is that this water baptism in *Jesus' name* actually *forgives sins* and promises that the baptized will *receive the gift of the Holy Spirit*. The point might be made clearer if we rephrased the prophecy in Luke 3 like this: "John baptized *only* with water, but Jesus will baptize with water *and* with the Holy Spirit." Or: "John baptized with water, but when Jesus' disciples baptize with water, Jesus will baptize with the Holy Spirit, too." Both baptisms employ water, but only the latter grants the promised forgiveness as well as the Holy Spirit, in Jesus' name.

As the rest of Acts unfolds, Luke goes to great trouble to emphasize the continuity of the water but the discontinuity of the Spirit in the two baptisms. He contrasts John's baptism with Christian baptism by juxtaposing Christian water baptism with the Holy Spirit again and again. He will, however, make it difficult to determine an exact sequence of receiving Christian water baptism and receiving the Holy Spirit. Why he does that will become clear later on.

Before we leave Acts 2, let us recall one more time that Jesus' two promises regarding the Holy Spirit were fulfilled on the day of Pentecost. First, the power of the Holy Spirit came upon the disciples to empower their mission into the world; and second, the Holy Spirit was promised and granted with water baptism in Jesus' name.

The next several chapters of Acts concern the disciples' ministry in and around Jerusalem to fellow Jews. It is only after the stoning of Stephen and the ensuing persecution of the nascent church that they begin to move farther afield. Philip is the pioneer: he travels to Samaria and starts preaching there.

The case of the Samaritans is a popular one for Classical Pentecostal accounts of baptism in the Holy Spirit, as it clearly indicates a time lapse between water baptism and the reception of the Holy Spirit. For Pentecostals, this indicates the difference between *conversion* ("But when they believed Philip as he preached good news about the kingdom of God and the name of Jesus Christ, they were baptized, both men and women," 8:12) and *Spirit baptism* ("Peter and John. . . came down and prayed for them that they might receive the Holy Spirit, for He had not yet fallen on any of them, but they had only been baptized in the name of the Lord Jesus. Then they laid their hands on them and they received the Holy Spirit," 8:14–17). This is taken to illustrate the Classical Pentecostal doctrine of subsequence: baptism in the Spirit is separate from and subsequent to conversion. To experience baptism in the Spirit is not to be saved. Rather, it is something that comes to people who have *already* been saved. Lutherans can appreciate the importance of that distinction: Pentecostals do not suggest that people need Spirit baptism to be saved, and thus they do not condemn those who have not experienced it as unsaved or un-Christian.

There are, however, some exegetical difficulties with the Classical Pentecostal position. Subsequence never stands alone but is nearly always in the company of two other teachings regarding Spirit baptism: speaking in tongues as initial evidence, and the missionary impetus of Spirit baptism and tongues. Thus, while the Samaritan story does illustrate "subsequence," no mention of speaking in tongues is made at all. Pentecostals will often say that tongues should be assumed or inferred here, since the gift is mentioned elsewhere in Acts (2:5–11, 10:46, 19:6). But if Luke wished to emphasize tongues as initial evidence, it seems a serious oversight to have left it out. Further, there is no hint that the gift of the Spirit upon the Samaritans was to empower *them* for mission. We hear nothing whatsoever of Samaritan missionaries.

On the other hand, if Lutherans (and other historic churches) wish to emphasize the link between Christian water baptism and the gift of the

Holy Spirit, why then the delay here? Why didn't the Spirit arrive in the same moment as water baptism? The Samaritan story seems to present as serious a problem to Lutheran teaching as it does to Pentecostal.

The confusion for both parties lies in losing sight of the larger drama of the first part of the book of Acts: namely, the drawing of all the estranged peoples of the earth into the fellowship of Israel through Jesus Christ. Thus, Luke's purpose in Acts 8 is not to talk either about tongues or about the sequence of water baptism and Spirit reception. His purpose is to validate Samaria as a legitimate part of the newborn church.

It is essential to realize that, until this point, *only Jews* have been drawn into the circle of Jesus' redemption. A lot of preaching about the Pentecost story in Acts 2 gets misled by the list of nations ("Parthians and Medes and Elamites" and so on), but actually the list refers to Jews in diaspora, not Gentiles. These Jews have moved far away from Judea, many of them apparently no longer understand Aramaic, some of them only manage to offer their sacrifices at the Jerusalem temple once in their lifetimes—but still, they are Jews. Pentecost was an exciting event not least of all because it linguistically reunited the people of Israel who had scattered to all corners of the earth and could no longer easily speak to one another.

But jump ahead to Acts 8 and we meet, much closer to the church's center in Jerusalem, the Samaritans. Remember the friction between Jews and Samaritans: they were close relatives, but that made their differences all the more painful. In John's Gospel (4:4–42), the disciples were surprised that Jesus would condescend to debate a Samaritan woman about competing Jewish and Samaritan religious claims. In Luke's Gospel, Jesus shocks his hearers by making the hero of one of his most famous parables a Samaritan, not a Jewish priest or a Jewish Levite (Luke 10:25–37). Jesus had alerted his disciples that the gospel would be proclaimed to all nations in a certain sequence: Jerusalem, Judea, Samaria, the end of the earth (Acts 1:8). What happens in Acts 8 is the extension of the mission from Jerusalem and Judea to Samaria—for the first time.

So Philip preaches, the people believe, and he baptizes them. Luke then indicates the surprising thing about this baptism: the Holy Spirit "had not yet fallen on any of them, but they had only been baptized in the name of the Lord Jesus." He makes sure you know *whose* baptism it is—Jesus', not John's—which is why it's so peculiar that the Holy Spirit "had not yet fallen." Meanwhile, word gets back to Jerusalem that the Samaritans have believed and been baptized, so the Jerusalem believers send Peter and John—the pillars and leaders of the church at this point—to Samaria to investigate just what Philip has been doing. Upon arrival, Peter and John pray for the Samaritans to receive the Holy Spirit and lay their hands upon them. Then and only then the Spirit does indeed arrive. Peter and John can now see for themselves that the Spirit has come upon the Samaritans, just as it did upon the Jewish disciples at Pentecost.

Acts 8 thus reports the first time a marginal, not-quite-Jewish group has been drawn into the community of believers. This fulfills Jesus' promise and foreshadows the much more dramatic inclusion of the Gentiles that will take place two chapters later. It's also worth noting that, after the inclusion of the Samaritans, Luke starts to offer other names for the believers in Jesus beyond the term "Israel": now they can also be called followers of "the Way" (9:2; 19:9 and 23; 22:4; 24:14 and 22), "Christians" (11:26), and "a people for His name" (15:14, which especially emphasizes the gathering of Gentiles). Believers in Jesus inhabit a dual reality: they are a part of Israel and yet they are more than and beyond Israel. Both realities are essential to the whole story of God's redemption.

The conclusion to draw from the Samaritan story, then, is that the Spirit was *exceptionally* delayed in order to establish the legitimacy of the Samaritans' place in the church. It's the only time in Acts that we hear of such a delay, in fact. The mission to the nations is the focus of the story—though not the missionary empowerment of the Samaritans themselves in any special way. While the baptism-Spirit relationship is not the main purpose of the story, the story of the Samaritans' inclusion does *assume* the close relationship that water baptism and the gift of the Spirit ought to have. The drama of the story would not work if that assumption were not already firmly in place.

This story has a fitting postscript: the baptism of a Jewish proselyte, namely the Ethiopian eunuch. Philip again is the apostle at hand to interpret the Scripture and then to baptize with water. Here nothing is said of the Holy Spirit or tongues or missionary empowerment at all, only of the water baptism itself. We should not infer therefore the absence of any of these things as the main point of the story. Rather, the point is the widening circle. Now an Ethiopian who is a Jewish proselyte has been drawn in, too.

We see the tight connection between water baptism and the gift of the Spirit again in the next chapter, which reports the conversion of Saul/Paul. When Ananias arrives in Damascus to visit the blinded persecutor of the church, he says, "Brother Saul, the Lord Jesus who appeared to you on the road by which you came has sent me so that you may regain your sight and be filled with the Holy Spirit" (9:17). Immediately, Luke tells us, the scales fall from Paul's eyes and he regains his sight—and his very first act is to get himself baptized, even before eating, although he has fasted for three days. Luke never tells us at which exact moment Paul's true conversion takes place or when exactly the Spirit falls on him. All he does is draw the connection again: the Spirit and water baptism go together.

Chapter 10 is a pivotal point in Acts, when the most monumental and consequential boundary is crossed. A pious man named Cornelius, who is a Roman centurion living in Caesarea, receives a message in prayer from an angel of God, telling him to find Simon Peter and hear what he has to say. Peter, meanwhile, is having a vision of his own, and an extremely disturbing one at that: a voice telling him to "kill and eat" (10:13) any number of animals that are unclean for observant Jews. Peter protests, but the vision repeats three times, insisting, "What God has made clean, do not call common" (10:15).

It is only once he has entered Cornelius's house that Peter begins to understand the dream: he and Cornelius are both human beings and both under God, and "in every nation anyone who fears Him and does what is right is acceptable to Him" (10:35). So Peter consents to share the gospel with Cornelius. He mentions how Jesus' ministry began "after the baptism that John proclaimed" (10:37) when God anointed Jesus "with the Holy Spirit and with power" (10:38)—notice again how the Holy Spirit distinguishes Jesus from John. Jesus healed people and liberated them from demons, was crucified, was raised from the dead by God, and has commanded the disciples to preach forgiveness of sins in his name (here again: Jesus' name vs. John's baptism) to everyone who believes in him.

What happens next startles everyone. "While Peter was still saying these things, the Holy Spirit fell on all who heard the word. And the believers from among the circumcised who had come with Peter were amazed, because the gift of the Holy Spirit was poured out even on the Gentiles. For they were hearing them speaking in tongues and extolling God. Then Peter declared, 'Can anyone withhold water for baptizing these people, who have received the Holy Spirit just as we have?' And he commanded them to be baptized in the name of Jesus Christ" (10:44–48).

Several things are worth noting here. One is that speaking in tongues and extolling God serve as an indication that the Holy Spirit has fallen on someone. The gift of tongues does function as one kind of "evidence," if not necessarily "initial evidence." In this story it appears to be a case of glossolalia rather than xenolalia (contrasting with Acts 2:5–11), lacking any particular missional orientation. Another thing to notice is the once-again tight connection between the Holy Spirit and water baptism. Because the Gentiles have received the Holy Spirit, Peter therefore *commands* them to be baptized. The order of events may be reversed from the day of Pentecost—at which time Peter spoke of water baptism in Jesus' name first, which would be followed by the Holy Spirit—but whatever the order, the two evidently belong together.

If the inclusion of the Samaritans was disturbing enough that Peter and John had to go and investigate, the inclusion of the Gentiles is an order of magnitude harder for the Jewish believers back home to accept. Accusations begin to fly the moment Peter arrives in Jerusalem. To counter their suspicions of his having flouted the law of Moses for no good reason, Peter recounts his dream and how he was brought to Cornelius's house. He concludes: "As I began to speak, the Holy Spirit fell on them just as on us at the beginning. And I remembered the word of the Lord, how he said, 'John baptized with water, but you will be baptized with the Holy Spirit.' If then God gave the same gift to them as he gave to us when we believed in the Lord Jesus Christ, who was I that I could stand in God's way?" (11:15–17).

Once again, the story highlights the contrast between John's baptism and Jesus'. Peter sees a perfect parallel between what happened to the Jews on Pentecost and what happened to the Gentiles at Caesarea. In fact, Jesus' prophecy of Pentecost in Acts 1 and Peter's recollection of the same prophecy in Acts 11 are the only two times that the phrase "baptized with the Holy Spirit" occurs in the whole book of Acts. Cornelius's conversion is a second Pentecost, this time for the Gentiles instead of for the Jews. Faith and reception of the *Holy Spirit* occurred in the same moment, and Peter sees that it would be wrong to withhold *water baptism* from them. Receiving the Holy Spirit is not an alternative to water baptism but all the more strongly urges it. Peter's accusers change their minds and rejoice instead: "Then to the Gentiles also God has granted repentance that leads to life" (11:18). *Repentance* is a key issue again, as it was for John, but this time the Holy Spirit is also a part of the equation.

The reception of the Holy Spirit by the Gentiles, as Peter witnessed with his own eyes, will ultimately resolve the controversy about their inclusion when it arises again in Acts 15 at the Jerusalem Council. Here it is finally and officially decided that the Gentiles have a part in the salvation promised to *Israel*.

Paul also stresses the contrast between John's baptism and the salvation that comes from Jesus. While preaching in the synagogue of Antioch in Pisidia, he reviews some of Israel's history and reminds the Jews of the promise to David of a savior. "Before his coming, John had proclaimed a baptism of repentance to all the people of Israel. And as John was finishing his course, he said, 'What do you suppose that I am? I am not he. No, but behold, after me one is coming, the sandals of whose feet I am not worthy to untie'" (13:24–25). This is all quite familiar: John deferring to Jesus and only being able to offer a baptism of repentance. But then after proclaiming the story of Jesus, Paul concludes, "through this man [Jesus] forgiveness of sins is proclaimed to you" (13:38)—something John had prophesied but could not himself provide.

The next baptisms we hear about in Acts are household baptisms: of Lydia and her household (16:11–15) and of the Philippian jailer and his household (16:25–34). Lutherans and other Christians who commend infant baptism have often cited these cases as implicit evidence for their practice: it seems fairly likely that a household in the ancient world would have included small children and babies, both of the family and of the servants or slaves.

Arguments from silence are not necessarily all that convincing, and many who deny infant baptism are indeed not convinced. Perhaps the more relevant point is that, in these cases, the head of the household makes the decision for baptism on behalf of the entire household—and that includes the adults! In other words, the adults receive baptism as a result of the head of the household's faith, not necessarily because of their own.

This point is emphasized particularly in the case of the Philippian jailer. He asks, "Sirs, what must I do to be saved?" Paul and Silas say to him, "Believe in the Lord Jesus, and you will be saved, you and your household" (16:30–31; "believe" and "will be saved" are both singular verbs). The apostles extend the scope of salvation beyond the jailer himself to include his household, even though the jailer alone is exhorted to believe. They then go to proclaim to the whole family and baptize everyone. When it's done, the jailer "rejoiced along with his entire household that he had believed in God" (16:34)—*he*, not *they*, though presumably *they* came to share in the faith *he* first had, if they were rejoicing. Throughout the story, however, the jailer's faith is the focus and cause of the whole household's baptism.

The case of the jailer and his household bears marked similarities to certain stories in Luke's Gospel, such as the paralytic being healed and forgiven on account of his friends' faith (Luke 5:17–26, especially v. 20) and the centurion's servant being healed on account of the centurion's faith (Luke 7:1–10). The faith of the friend or of the head of the household is not meant as an alternative to the faith of the others. But God hears and responds to these believers' requests for the salvation of others. In Acts, such faith is sufficient cause for the baptism of others in the household, which itself should give rise to faith in these baptized people. This is the logic behind infant baptisms at the request of believing parents and godparents.

Another contrast between John's baptism and Christian baptism surfaces in Acts 18:24–28. Here we learn about a Jew named Apollos visiting Ephesus. Luke heaps praises upon him: "He was an eloquent man, competent in the Scriptures. He had been instructed in the way of the Lord. And being fervent in spirit, he spoke and taught accurately the things concerning Jesus." There was just one problem: "he knew only the baptism of John." From Luke's perspective, Apollos really must have been an extraordinary preacher to be absolved of such a serious oversight. The story goes on: "He began to speak boldly in the synagogue, but when Priscilla and Aquila heard him, they took him aside and explained to him the way of God more accurately." Apollos evidently accepted the correction and earned even more admiration from his fellow Christians: "And when he wished to cross to Achaia, the brothers encouraged him and wrote to the disciples to welcome him. When he arrived, he greatly helped those who through grace had believed, for he powerfully refuted the Jews in public, showing by the Scriptures that the Christ was Jesus." This story demonstrates how long the confusion over John's and Jesus' baptisms persisted, and why Luke had to work so hard in his history to distinguish them from one another. Even a great evangelist like Apollos was in need of "more accurate" information to supplement his own.

The final account of baptism in Acts (other than Paul remembering his own in 22:16) is that of the Ephesian disciples in ch. 19. Every other time Luke uses the word "disciples," he means it as a term of approval for Jesus' followers. But the Ephesians are an unusual case. When Paul approaches them, he asks, "Did you receive the Holy Spirit when you believed?" They respond, "No, we have not even heard that there is a Holy Spirit!" (19:2). From Luke's perspective, that is an extremely strange response. How could anyone believe in Jesus and yet not know about the Holy Spirit? This prompts Paul to inquire, "Into what then were you baptized?" His assumption is that, if they are believers, then they must have been baptized. Their answer: "Into John's baptism" (19:3).

That explains it. As we've seen all along, John's baptism was for repentance, but it did not bestow the Holy Spirit. The Ephesian disciples shared in John's repentance and expectation of the Messiah, but they didn't realize that the Messiah had actually come, or that he'd sent his Holy Spirit upon believers, either. Perhaps that is not altogether surprising. After all, Ephesus is a very long way from the Judean countryside, and news may have been slow to travel. But their example does show how widespread the John the Baptist movement was in the ancient world. In fact, even today there are followers of John the Baptist who do not accept Jesus as the Messiah: the Mandaeans of Iraq.

So Paul's job is to bring the Ephesians up to date. "John baptized with the baptism of repentance, telling the people to believe in the one who was to come after him, that is, Jesus" (19:4). On hearing this, the Ephesians are baptized in the name of Jesus. This is not a "rebaptism" in the Christian sense, since the first baptism was not Christian at all, but John's. The baptism is followed by the laying-on of hands, the Holy Spirit comes upon them, and they begin to speak in tongues and prophesy. Here again we see the recurring themes: repentance; the distinction between John's water baptism and Christian water baptism; the close alignment of Christian water baptism and the Holy Spirit; and the familiar though not mandatory features of the laying-on of hands and speaking in tongues. As was the case with the Samaritan believers, the laying-on of hands by Paul the apostle signifies how the Ephesian disciples of John have now made a full and legitimate entry into the community of the church.

And that is where Luke's story of ingathering comes to an end. The Jews, the Samaritans, the proselytes, the Gentiles, and finally the disciples of John have all received Christian baptism and been given the gift of the Holy Spirit. All communities, if not all individuals, are accounted for. After ch. 19, Acts takes a different turn, narrating Paul's confrontation with the Roman political authorities that will eventually take him to his martyr's death.

Two thousand years later, it is simply taken for granted by Christians that John the Baptist was the forerunner prophet making Israel ready for the Messiah. It never occurs to us that there might have been a rivalry between

John and Jesus or between their followers. But recall that John had to send his disciples to ask Jesus whether he was the one or if John should wait for another—yet this happened *after* Jesus' baptism, complete with the descent of the Holy Spirit and the words from heaven! In response, Jesus recounts his miracles to John's disciples: "the blind receive their sight, the lame walk, lepers are cleansed, and the deaf hear, the dead are raised up, the poor have good news preached to them"—but his concluding words are sharp: "And blessed is the one who is not offended by me" (Luke 7:22–23). It is not impossible to imagine that the stringent preacher of repentance might have had his doubts about the one who worked mercy and forgave sins. And it is not hard to imagine that John's disciples might have struggled to transfer their loyalty over to Jesus, even after their beloved leader was beheaded.

The quiet and long-forgotten competition between John and Jesus, or at least between their disciples, may also explain why Luke, alone of all the Evangelists, offers an extended narrative of John's conception and birth. It is important to Luke to show right from the start how John prepares the way for the Lord but is not, himself, the final word. The contrast between their parents—Zechariah who doubts and Mary who believes—further indicates the relative importance of the two figures.

To conclude: John's water baptism was taken up by Jesus and his disciples and transformed into a new thing. But the earliest Christians were so influenced by John's preaching that the transformation from John's baptism to Christian baptism might not have been immediately apparent to them. Luke's purpose is to show where the one baptism ends and the other begins—namely, in the giving of the Holy Spirit and the forgiveness of sins.

Now that we have taken this tour through Acts and seen Luke's main concerns—a depiction of the lively work of the Spirit in the early church, the distinction between John's baptism and Christian baptism, and the gradual ingathering of all the peoples of the earth into the salvation that God sent to Israel—we can start putting specifically Lutheran and Pentecostal questions to it. That will be the topic of the next chapter.

For Further Reading

Oscar Cullmann, *Baptism in the New Testament*, trans. J. K. S. Reid (London: SCM, 1950) is a classic study by a well-regarded Lutheran biblical scholar.

James Dunn, *Baptism in the Holy Spirit: A Re-examination of the New Testament Teaching on the Gift of the Spirit in Relation to Pentecostalism Today* (Nashville: Westminster John Knox, 1977) is the most sustained critical argument against the Pentecostal understanding of Spirit baptism from an Evangelical/Reformed perspective. Many Pentecostal books and articles have been written in response; one that reviews all of these Pentecostal counter-arguments and endorses them is William P. Atkinson, *Baptism in the Spirit: Luke-Acts and the Dunn Debate* (Eugene: Pickwick, 2011).

CHAPTER 5

Baptism II

THE BIBLICAL WRITERS HAVE their own concerns. They testify to what they have seen and heard and what God has revealed to them. But as the church continues its course through history, new questions and experiences and difficulties arise. Somehow they have to be analyzed and dealt with in a way that is faithful to the Scripture, even if the Scripture does not deal with them directly. That's where the fine art of interpretation comes in. That's what we have to do now.

We've alluded to some of the differences of interpretation between Pentecostals and Lutherans in the previous chapter, but now we will delve into them more deeply. A number of questions arise concerning the meaning and practice of water baptism and of what Pentecostals call Spirit baptism.

So to get back to the question that launched the previous chapter: is baptism in the Spirit something different from Christian baptism in water?

When Classical Pentecostals use the term "baptism in the Holy Spirit," they definitely mean something different from Christian water baptism. Spirit baptism refers to a post-conversion experience of the Holy Spirit, and it certainly is an *experience*, not something that could happen to you without your noticing it. It generally comes through prayer, the laying-on of hands, and "tarrying," often in the context of worship with other Christians. A desire to obey and to yield oneself to God's will is crucial. Thus, this is an experience that happens only to believers, not to unbelievers, though it is possible that faith and Spirit baptism will arrive in the same moment. While all believing Christians have the Spirit, baptism in the Spirit is distinguished from ordinary Christian possession of the Spirit because it is an "enduement" of power for the sake of missionary witness. Speaking in tongues was seen as the evidence of a genuine Spirit baptism in early American Pentecostalism, but today many Pentecostals argue that any manifestation of a charismatic gift can serve as evidence of Spirit baptism, and most Pentecostals have recognized that a person who speaks in tongues at the moment of Spirit baptism may not necessarily go on speaking in tongues but receive a different spiritual gift instead. Clearly, then, Pentecostals take John's and Jesus' distinction between baptizing in water and baptizing in the Holy Spirit to be about categorically different events, rather than the contrast between John's water baptism *without the Spirit* and Jesus' or Jesus' disciples' water baptism *with the Spirit.*

As is evident from the account given in the previous chapter, this is very likely a misreading of Luke's intent. The association of Christian water baptism with the gift of the Holy Spirit is very strong throughout Acts, while tongues and missional empowerment are not mentioned in every account of the reception of the Spirit. The kind of tongues most useful for mission work, namely xenolalia, occurs only on the day of Pentecost itself, not after. The exact phrase "baptized in the Holy Spirit" is used only twice in Acts: prophesying the Pentecost event (1:5) and recalling the Gentiles' reception of the Spirit (11:16). However, many other terms are used interchangeably with "baptized in the Holy Spirit" throughout Acts: "received" (2:38, 8:17, 10:47, 19:2); "come upon" (1:8, 19:6), "filled" (2:4); "poured out" (2:33, 10:45); "fell" (10:44, 11:15); "given" (5:32, 15:8). These various verbs are often used to describe the same event, so no sharp distinction is made between them as if they were technical terms. Sometimes the Spirit is the subject of the action ("fell," "came upon") and sometimes the object ("received," "given," "poured out").

It helps at this point to recall a bit of early Pentecostal history. Before Azusa Street, "baptism in the Holy Spirit" was a term in use among Holiness Christians. In a certain sense, it was a term in search of a definition. There was a great deal of dispute about what it really meant. Some took it to be synonymous with sanctification. The break of Pentecostals from the Holiness movement came from their identifying "baptism in the Holy Spirit" with a dramatic experience of missionary empowerment.

By the same token, it could be said that the Pentecostal experience was an experience in search of a name and a justification. It's impossible to overestimate the hostility, mockery, and rejection on the part of other Christians toward early Pentecostals. These others were often quite determined to conclude that Pentecostals were demon-possessed or delusional. Thus, an appeal to a biblically verifiable experience by use of a term already in circulation was a good way for Pentecostals to establish the legitimacy of what they were experiencing.

Finally, it should be noted that most of the early adherents of the Pentecostal movement came from Christian traditions that had rejected infant baptism and practiced believer's baptism instead. (Some notable exceptions were certain early German Pentecostals associated with Lutheran pastor Jonathan Paul and certain early English Pentecostals associated with Anglican pastor Alexander A. Boddy.) The rejection of infant baptism was partly a result of a longstanding anti-Catholicism and partly a denunciation of lukewarm or unbelieving Christians who had been baptized as infants. In churches that practice believer's baptism exclusively, baptism is not considered sacramental or saving but is a voluntary act of obedience, offering testimony to one's faith and commitment to discipleship. It would therefore *always* be subsequent to faith in Christ, *always* subsequent to some kind of encounter with or reception of the Holy Spirit. It would not have made a great deal of sense to talk about the Holy Spirit as something received with water baptism or in infancy when people were coming to faith before baptism, sometimes long before.

In light of our exegesis of Luke-Acts, one of the principal problems with this Pentecostal distinctive is its terminology. A unique experience called "baptism in the Holy Spirit," which is separate from water baptism and mandates the specific qualifiers of tongues (or other charismatic gifts) and a missionary empowerment, isn't sustainable from the text. A further difficulty is that, throughout the New Testament, Christian baptism signifies an entrance or a beginning, and furthermore one that is common to every believer (for example, Rom 6:3–4, I Cor 12:13, Gal 3:27, and Col 2:12). Thus to use the term "baptism" to designate an experience that usually happens later in one's Christian life, and evidently not to everyone but only to some, obscures the fundamental meaning of Christian baptism as something that marks the beginning of a person's life in the salvation of Jesus. Luke-Acts associates Christian water baptism with the reception of the Holy Spirit and does not describe a separate, distinct, later experience of "baptism in the Spirit" serving another purpose.

It would be a severe mistake, however, to conclude that a misapplied term or reified experience means that all Pentecostals who have had a powerful experience of the Spirit are simply deluded or demon-possessed, as the first critics concluded. Here we need to confront some of the obstacles to understanding on the part of Lutherans (and other historic Christians).

One is simple defensiveness. Lutherans who see the vivid faith of Pentecostals put into action through energetic missions may be embarrassed at the lukewarm indifference of many of their own. A form of Christianity that expects testimony and discipleship is probably going to make a (for instance) state-church or folk-church Christianity, where membership in the church is often more a cultural than a spiritual matter, look bad if not outright unfaithful. A quick defense of infant baptism and a rejection of all powerful experiences of the Holy Spirit might well have nothing to do with genuine theological or biblical engagement but may simply be a cover-up for faithlessness.

Another real obstacle is a post-Enlightenment rejection of all things supernatural. It is one thing to engage with real scientific progress in explaining how the universe works, or to use such scientific discoveries to unmask superstitions. But it is quite another thing to turn science into a positivistic philosophy that rules out, as a matter of principle, any real experience of God or the activity of God within creation. The Lutheran Confessions assert that God is real, living, and active; that He has created and continues to sustain all that He has made; that He has called and interacted with various persons throughout history, from Abraham to Moses to the prophets to the apostles; that He became flesh in Jesus Christ, performed miracles, was crucified, and rose from the dead. The plot of the book of Acts is the outward-moving, ever-surprising activity of the Holy Spirit in claiming sinners for salvation through Jesus Christ. Lutherans cannot simply reject Pentecostal claims to experience this same Spirit on the grounds that it isn't possible. To do so is to deny their own Confessional and biblical convictions.

There are also burdens within Lutheran history that tend to foster a suspicious reaction toward Pentecostal claims. The twin evils of elitism, symbolized by medieval monks and nuns trying to justify themselves through superior living, and Enthusiasm, symbolized by the *Schwärmer* who "devoured the Holy Spirit feathers and all,"[1] loom over every Lutheran conversation about Pentecostal matters. Here again it is necessary to test the spirits (I Thess 5:19–21, I John 4:1).

The initial Pentecostal impetus was not to create an elite but, quite the contrary, to democratize, along the lines of Joel's prophecy quoted by Peter in Acts 2:17–18: "And in the last days it shall be, God declares, that I will pour out my Spirit on all flesh, and your sons and your daughters

1. Luther, "Against the Heavenly Prophets," in *Luther's Works*, 83.

shall prophesy, and your young men shall see visions, and your old men shall dream dreams; even on my male servants and female servants in those days I will pour out my Spirit, and they shall prophesy." All Christians were invited by the early Pentecostals to seek Spirit baptism, and it was believed that all Christians could and should receive it. Spirit baptism was not a requirement for salvation but a gift freely offered to the already-saved. It broke down gender barriers, it broke down color barriers, and it broke down lay-clergy barriers, long before social and political activism began to do so in wider society. It gave a voice—the voice of tongues, prophecy, or knowledge—to those who had been habitually silenced in the church. Liturgy was less strictly ordered in order to offer a space and a role to all comers, not only the clergy. The Spirit-baptized were not to be set apart but to become the norm.

That doesn't mean it necessarily happened. All Christian communities struggle with the failure to live up to their own ideals, and neither Lutherans nor Pentecostals are exceptions. The Pew Forum on Religion and Public Life found that nearly half of U.S. Pentecostals report that they never speak in tongues.[2] There can be unpleasant power struggles when those who have been Spirit-baptized assert their authority while eschewing education or community discipline. There is no need to idealize the Pentecostal reality. But it is essential to see that Pentecostalism is not fundamentally aiming toward spiritual superiority but rather toward a universal Christian experience of being filled with and empowered by the Holy Spirit for the sake of the gospel.

Analogously, baptism in the Spirit has never been taken by Pentecostals to be an alternative to reading, understanding, or obeying the Scripture. The accusation of being Enthusiasts, though nearly automatic with Lutherans, misses the mark. Pentecostals tend to have such a profound regard for the Bible that it puts most Lutherans to shame! Prophecies and words of knowledge that emerge in worship or privately are always to be tested against the Scripture, and if found to be in contradiction they are rejected. In any event, such prophecies are not of the new-revelation sort, as if Pentecostals supposed they were adding to or altering the biblical foundation. They are most often words of encouragement or sometimes rebuke directed toward specific local communities, interpreting and applying the Scripture to the local context. Pentecostals who break away from the scriptural rule can expect to come in for grave condemnation by their fellows. Again, this

2. Gaines, "Study: Many Pentecostals Don't Speak in Tongues," 18.

doesn't mean that Lutherans (or even other Pentecostals) will agree with every interpretation of the Bible or evaluate all prophecies in the exact same way. It only means that a contemptuous dismissal of Pentecostals as favoring extra-biblical revelations is simply wrong.

What, then, is going on with Pentecostals, if not "baptism in the Spirit"?

As it turns out, the book of Acts supplies plenty of templates for Pentecostal experience quite apart from Pentecost itself or other reports of the gift of tongues. The Spirit is certainly at work in water baptism in Jesus' name, but the Spirit is not *only* at work in water baptism in Jesus' name! Take, for example, this account from Acts 4:23–31, not long after the day of Pentecost and directly after Peter and John's confrontation with the religious authorities:

> When they were released, they went to their friends and reported what the chief priests and the elders had said to them. And when they heard it, they lifted their voices together to God and said, "Sovereign Lord, who made the heaven and the earth and the sea and everything in them, who through the mouth of our father David, your servant, said by the Holy Spirit, 'Why did the Gentiles rage, and the peoples plot in vain? The kings of the earth set themselves, and the rulers were gathered together, against the Lord and against his Anointed'—for truly in this city there were gathered together against your holy servant Jesus, whom you anointed, both Herod and Pontius Pilate, along with the Gentiles and the peoples of Israel, to do whatever your hand and your plan had predestined to take place. And now, Lord, look upon their threats and grant to your servants to continue to speak your word with all boldness, while you stretch out your hand to heal, and signs and wonders are performed through the name of your holy servant Jesus." And when they had prayed, the place in which they were gathered together was shaken, and they were all filled with the Holy Spirit and continued to speak the word of God with boldness.

This sounds remarkably like Pentecostal descriptions of their encounters with the Spirit. Believers gather together in an intense fellowship of prayer and beg God for the strength and boldness to bear testimony to the world. God responds with dramatic signs (the house itself shakes!), the people are filled with the Holy Spirit, and they are empowered to continue on their mission. Peter and John had already received the Holy Spirit before this moment (Luke affirms that Peter in front of the authorities was "filled with the Holy Spirit," Acts 4:8), but here they receive the Spirit *again* or *afresh*, with a specific missional orientation—no surprise, since mission is Luke's overall agenda in Acts. Stephen speaks by the Spirit against his opponents in the synagogue; the Spirit prompts Philip to talk to the Ethiopian eunuch and then whisks him away to Azotus to continue his itinerant preaching; the Spirit sets Paul and Barnabas apart for mission among the Gentiles in Antioch and Cyprus but prevents them from going to Bithynia. Reception of the Spirit isn't a one-time event. The Spirit will come whenever the need arises.

We can say, then, that the early Pentecostals were certainly correct to believe that spiritual gifts like tongues and prophecy were intended by Luke-Acts to be a part of ordinary Christian existence (Paul thought so, too; see I Cor 12–14); that the Holy Spirit continues to work and be active in spurring missions to places where the gospel has never been preached; and that the Spirit can be experienced perceptibly by the faithful rather than remaining the "silent partner" we officially confess but otherwise know nothing about. It is unfortunate that all these correct interpretations of the Spirit in Luke-Acts got linked to the term "baptism" and were defined strictly as a particular kind of experience with evidential features. But that should not blind us to the genuine insights that Pentecostals have reintroduced to a church that has long since forgotten them.

Even though we have good cause to affirm the link between the Holy Spirit and water baptism, some serious questions still need to be addressed—questions that will certainly come up in conversation between Lutherans and Pentecostals. Are all baptized people automatically saved? Why are the Holy Spirit and water baptism linked in Acts but not presented in an exact and unvarying sequence? What is the reason for preferring infant baptism or at least accepting it as a legitimate Christian baptism? And is it ever acceptable to "rebaptize" those who received Christian baptism as infants?

It would be fair to accept the critique that Lutherans, like other churches that practice infant baptism, have misread the import of Christian water baptism at times. This is especially the case when baptism has been treated like a fail-safe ritual guaranteeing salvation without any concern for the living faith that should result from it. The practice of believer's baptism arose among the Anabaptists in the sixteenth century (right in the midst of the Reformation) in part as a protest against the automatic, ritualistic baptism of all infants amidst total neglect of instruction in the faith or any personal commitment.

Even while Acts puts the Holy Spirit and water baptism together, it nevertheless stresses that even baptized believers who have received the Holy Spirit are capable of falling away. Two stories illustrate this: Ananias and Sapphira, and Simon Magus.

In the former case, the snare of wealth and the desire to look holier than they really are lead this married couple to pretend that they have given all the proceeds of the sale of their property to the apostles, when in fact they have withheld some of it (5:1–11). Both are accused of lying to or testing the Holy Spirit, despite the fact that they would have already been baptized and received the Spirit as part of the Christian community. When exposed in their lies, they each fall down dead.

In the latter case, Luke clearly states that Simon Magus ("the magician") believed Philip's preaching and got baptized, and he was with the others when Peter and John arrived to pray for the gift of the Spirit upon the Samaritans. Despite baptism and faith, though, Simon had not fully appreciated the new dimensions of his Christian existence, because he asked if he could buy the Spirit from Peter! (This is where we get the term "simony," the buying and selling of clerical offices.) We only know that Simon was reprimanded, not whether he changed his ways afterward. These two stories together are proof that neither baptism nor faith functions as a foolproof guarantee against sin and error.

This fact, together with the lack of any unvarying sequence of water baptism and the bestowal of the Spirit (either might precede the other), is Luke's testimony to the sovereign freedom of the Spirit. God cannot be cornered and demanded to perform. Long before Peter even thinks of baptizing Gentiles, the Spirit simply shows up and claims Cornelius. Acts wants to show the reader that the Spirit of God is at work among the disciples and headed out toward the nations to proclaim the gospel of Jesus Christ and the forgiveness of sins. Neither human responses of faith nor human rites (even as important as baptism) lead the way; only the Spirit does, freely using such means as testimony and miracles and baptism. Peter says in Acts 2:39, "For the promise is for you and for your children and for all who are far off, everyone *whom the Lord our God calls to himself.*" Acts 2:47 emphasizes that "*the Lord added* to their number day by day those who were being saved." In both verses, the point is clear: faith and salvation are *God's* work, first and foremost, whether in adults or children, whether in people close to the Jerusalem center of Jesus' action or far from it.

While Luke's Gospel depicts many personal encounters between Jesus and various individuals, Acts has a more global perspective. Its agenda is to report and legitimate the movement of the gospel from Jerusalem to all Judea and to Samaria and ultimately to the end of the earth, as Jesus promised in 1:8. Therefore, to try to extract a sequence of salvific or empowering experiences on the *personal* level from the book of Acts is to miss the bigger picture. Note that after Luke has seen to the ingathering of the Jews (Acts 2), the Samaritans and a Jewish proselyte (Acts 8), the Gentiles (Acts 10), and finally John's disciples (Acts 19), there is no more talk of the Holy Spirit being given. In fact, there's very little talk of the Holy Spirit at all after that point. The job has been done: all the estranged groups have been claimed, the original Jewish core of disciples has come to terms with the redefinition of the people of God, and it's time to move on to another concern—namely, Paul's confrontation with the political authorities.

If Luke imagines any temporal sequence of events or experiences at all, it is that the Spirit moves *first* to bring the news of the gospel to a person or a community. Everything else flows out of that, in whatever order accomplishes the Spirit's purpose. Acts is the story of the outward traveling of the gospel, which makes everything else possible: faith, repentance, baptism, reception of the Spirit—ultimately, salvation.

In the matter of infant vs. believer's baptism, the first consideration is that the New Testament cannot imagine an unbaptized Christian. If you are a believer in Jesus, then the first thing you will do is get yourself baptized (think of Paul after Ananias's visit). How are we to determine at what exact moment a child raised among believers—praying, worshiping, and singing with them, hearing Bible stories from them, enjoying their fellowship— "really" starts to believe? When a child is born into a Christian family and raised within the church, it is profoundly artificial to deny baptism until a later age, if baptism is properly understood as the beginning of a person's inclusion in Jesus' salvation.

If that's the case, why isn't Scripture clearer about it? We can call this the second-generation problem of interpretation. Most of the New Testament is written to, by, and about people who encounter Jesus and the gospel for the first time *as adults*. That's hardly surprising in a new religious movement. But the circumstances will be different for the children born to those converts and raised in the faith. The "conversion," if that is even the right word for it, of these children will not resemble what it was for their parents. Infant baptism is a practice for the second (or later) generation, for children who have never known any faith but that of Jesus, whose beginning with Jesus took place in the bosom of the family.

Recognized or not, this is an issue for Pentecostal and other believer's-baptism churches. It is evident that many children raised in believer's-baptism churches end up choosing baptism out of peer pressure, parental expectation, or other less-than-pure motives. Sometimes the extreme emphasis on personal confession has caused people who received baptism after a testimony of faith to seek a second baptism when they come to a newer and deeper level of faith—or even a third, or a fourth. But multiple Christian baptisms have no scriptural precedent whatsoever. Infant baptism, however, corresponds to the Gospel stories of healing (in Luke, "healing" and "saving" are the same word) and the Acts accounts of household baptisms. It affirms that God responds to the requests of believers for the salvation of another. The ultimate goal is, of course, that the one so saved will come to faith, too. But here again the emphasis is on God's prior work to which we respond, not our prior work to which God responds.

On the other hand, it is clear that in all too many locales infant baptism has been reduced to a rite of welcoming the child to the family, not committing its life to Jesus. In such circumstances, there may be a place for the conscientious delay of baptism as its own kind of witness to the gravity of dying and rising with Christ. There is no advantage gained in being baptized as an infant if one's parents or wider community have no interest in teaching and professing the Christian faith. Baptism was never intended by the apostolic writers (or Luther) as an *alternative* to faith, but as its solid ground, as God's first act toward one's salvation. Luther teaches in the Large Catechism that baptism indeed saves, but it is of no benefit to a baptized person who does not have faith in the offered salvation. Honesty demands that pastors not accede to requests for infant baptism if they know that the parents have no faith or no intention of raising the child in the church.

Lutherans would also do well to reflect on mission situations—the very kind that Luke talks about in Acts—where adults hear of the gospel for the first time and so request baptism for themselves. Much Lutheran teaching on baptism simply assumes infant baptism, but that is not so much the standard anymore. A deeper reflection on the connection between God's acts in baptism and creating faith, and the human act of confession, could be the happy result of conversation with Pentecostals on exactly these issues.

Finally, there is the thorny question of rebaptism. Probably nothing else causes such anger and mistrust between divided Christians. From a Lutheran perspective, any baptism that is done by a Christian community with water and in the name of the Father, Son, and Holy Spirit is a legitimate baptism and must not under any circumstances be repeated. This is because Lutherans understand baptism to be God's act, not merely a human one. As Luther explains in the Large Catechism, "To be baptized in God's name is to be baptized not by human beings but by God himself. Although it is performed by human hands, it is nevertheless truly God's own act."[3] To repeat such a baptism is to suggest that God's action was invalid or powerless. It does not matter in which church the baptism took place; as long as it was performed with water and in the trinitarian name, Lutherans recognize it as a true baptism, including in the case of converts from one Christian church to another.

Of course, the difficulty is that most Pentecostals do not regard baptism in the same way that Lutherans do. Following a theological orientation that dates as far back as sixteenth-century Anabaptists, and mirrors later Baptist and Evangelical practice, Pentecostals tend to see baptism primarily as an obedient act of public testimony. Submitting to water baptism is, for them, a human witness to one's own conversion, which may be understood as God's act, a human decision, or both. With this understanding of baptism, we can see why they would consider infant baptism worthless: the infant did not and could not make a public confession of faith. (Whether the infant could even have faith is yet another question. Luther argued that it was not impossible and cited John the Baptist leaping in Elizabeth's womb, in recognition of Jesus in Mary's womb, as proof.) The Lutheran Confessions put the emphasis instead on God's action: "[S]acraments were instituted not only to be marks of profession among human beings but much more to be signs and testimonies of God's will toward us, intended to arouse and strengthen faith in those who use them."[4]

But because of the emphasis on personal confession rather than God's sign, it is not uncommon for Pentecostals to invite Christians who were

---

3. Luther, "The Large Catechism," in *The Book of Concord*, 457.

4. Melanchthon, "The Augsburg Confession," Article XIII, in *The Book of Concord*, 47.

baptized as infants in other churches to get baptized—not "again," since they don't recognize the infant baptism—but "for the first time." The emphasis is on the human act of obedience to the command to be baptized. Yet quite often there is no mutual recognition of baptism between different Pentecostal churches, especially of the Neocharismatic type, which means that a Christian moving from church to church may request and receive, or be required to receive, multiple Christian baptisms. It is hard as a Lutheran to react to this with anything other than horror.

While no immediate solution lies at hand, we can take steps on both sides to reduce the scandal. Lutherans and other historic churches that practice infant baptism must commit to doing so faithfully: that is, they must baptize children only within the faith community of the church, not as a cultural ritual for unbelieving parents or "fire insurance" for superstitious parents who otherwise have nothing to do with the church. This is not to suggest a hard or judgmental attitude, but to encourage wise pastoral discernment. The birth of a child is often an occasion for parents to return to the church after a long lapse. Every effort should be made to catechize and welcome the parents back into the community of the faithful. They should be prepared to make their own vows as parents and godparents in good faith; clergy do not want to be in the position of leading parents into making vows before God that they have no intention of keeping. The claim for the legitimacy of infant baptism is undermined, if not altogether invalidated, every time Lutherans baptize infants apart from the faith of the church, the parents, and the godparents.

At the same time, Lutherans should take any opportunity that arises to ask Pentecostals and other believer-baptizers not to repeat the act of baptism in the case of an infant-baptized person's conversion or move to a Pentecostal church. Many Pentecostals already recognize the urgency of reconsidering their own practice in this regard. As one Pentecostal theologian, Frank D. Macchia, writes: "This problem is especially acute in countries where a good part of the population may be infant baptized but absent from the life of the church or active faith in Christ. . . [T]he Pentecostals in such contexts should be cognizant of the fact that such infant-baptized persons not currently active in the church have already in a profound sense been laid claim to by God in the bosom of the historic church. Evangelism should not proceed without recognition of this fact."[5] A convert can certainly make a public profession of faith, which is the key concern in most

5. Macchia, *Baptized in the Spirit*, 73.

believer's-baptism settings anyway. This can be viewed as a "completion" of the water baptism that began in infancy.

Indeed, there is a parallel element in the Lutheran practice of confirmation, in which the act of baptism not chosen in infancy is publicly affirmed in adulthood after instruction in the faith. Lutherans would do well also to consider options for infant-baptized persons in their own churches who have experienced, later in life, a dramatic reorientation to the gospel. It would be helpful to offer them opportunities to make public witness of that fact, though of course without rebaptism.

Not indiscriminately baptizing infants, and not rebaptizing the infant-baptized, will decrease the tension and increase the mutual respect between divided churches, enabling mutually edifying conversations that will otherwise remain nearly impossible.

For Further Reading

From Luther, the most valuable writings on baptism are the section on "Baptism" in the Large Catechism and the treatise "Concerning Rebaptism," which can be found in *Luther's Works*, American Edition, 55 vols., eds. J. Pelikan and H. Lehmann (St. Louis and Philadelphia: Concordia and Fortress, 1955ff.), 40:229–62.

The best-known ecumenical document, "Baptism, Eucharist and Ministry," which was drafted by the Faith and Order Commission and approved in 1982, has a very good discussion of the respective views of infant-baptism and believer's-baptism traditions, with suggestions for peaceable coexistence. A follow-up document of equal interest is "One Baptism: Toward Mutual Recognition," Faith and Order Paper No. 210. Both can easily be found online.

Bryan Holstrom, *Infant Baptism and the Silence of the New Testament* (Greenville: Ambassador International, 2008) argues from a Reformed perspective that the "silence" of the New Testament on infant baptism does not disqualify infant baptism but in fact commends it. He also takes into account early church and Reformation practice regarding infant baptism.

Terje Hegertun, "Bridge over Troubled Water? Rebaptism in a Nordic Context—Reflections and Proposals," *Pneuma* 35/2 (2013) 235–52 argues from a Pentecostal perspective for a careful reevaluation of the requirement of rebaptism for infant-baptized (in his context, mainly Lutheran) persons who wish to become members of Pentecostal churches.

CHAPTER 6

Charismata

FOR PENTECOSTALS, A POWERFUL encounter with the Holy Spirit entails a bestowal of divine gifts of new powers and abilities. They are personally enriching, to be sure, but their primary purpose is the building-up of the church, both through missional outreach and congregational edification. The most common term to describe these gifts is *charismata* (singular: *charisma*), a transliteration of the Greek term that Paul uses for divine gifts.

Paul appears to have invented the term "charisma" himself. It has virtually no counterpart in any other Greek literature of his period or before. It derives from the Greek word *charis*, which means "grace," so charismata can be understood to mean "graced-things." You can also see the word *charis* hiding in one of the terms for the Lord's Supper: eu*charis*t, which has the more specific meaning of "thanksgiving."

Paul doesn't use the word "charisma" only for the powers or abilities bestowed on human beings by God. He applies it to other divine gifts as well. So, for example, we read in Romans: "For the wages of sin is death, but the free gift [*charisma*] of God is eternal life in Christ Jesus our Lord" (6:23). On another occasion, Paul uses the word to describe the gift of his deliverance from prison: "You also must help us by prayer, so that many will give thanks on our behalf for the blessing [*charisma*] granted us through the prayers of many" (II Cor 1:11). In these cases, the word charisma can be used interchangeably with other Greek words for gift, like *dōron* and *dōrēma*.

Paul sometimes uses another term to describe the powers bestowed on people by God, *pneumatika*. This word means literally "spiritual-things," deriving from *pneuma*, which means "spirit." *Pneumatika* seems, though, to be the term that the Corinthians themselves liked to use, rather than the one Paul himself preferred (namely, charismata). Sometimes the two terms are combined to make the phrase *charisma pneumatikōn*, "spiritual gift," as in Romans 1:11. For simplicity's sake, we'll stick with the term "charisma" in this chapter.

Many New Testament books refer to such things as healing and prophecy being given to human beings, including the Gospels, Hebrews, James, I John, and Revelation. Acts depicts such spiritual gifts as prophecy, speaking in tongues, healing, exhortation, miracles, teaching, discernment, and administration. But these books do not label the charismata with a collective term nor do they analyze their meaning. Paul does both, however, and at great length, so we will turn our attention now to I Corinthians, where his most extensive discussion of the topic may be found. The discussion here is addressed primarily to Lutherans who have little-to-no experience of the charismata and don't know what to think about them. Lutherans already familiar with the charismata will nevertheless perhaps find things of value here.

The first thing Paul has to say about the Corinthians in his first letter to them is that they "are not lacking in any gift [charismati]" (1:7a), for which Paul gives thanks to God. But immediately thereafter he launches into a many-chapters-long discussion of all the Corinthians' failures as a church. There are schisms among them. They claim loyalty to different apostles but then make themselves out to be better than the apostles. They go in search of worldly wisdom but ignore divine wisdom. They tolerate sexual immorality within the community and at the same time denounce marriage. They have disputes with each other and then expect the pagan legal authorities to settle the case in court. They proudly eat meat offered to idols with no concern over scandalizing weak consciences, all the while allowing their celebrations of the Lord's Supper to degenerate into a display of wealth and poverty.

In short, the Corinthians have heard and accepted the good news about Jesus's death and resurrection, but they have grasped almost none of the consequences of that news for their life together. They are still operating according to human wisdom, being mere infants in Christ who can only take milk but not yet any solid food. What they need is to be taught by the Spirit.

> Now we have received not the spirit of the world, but the Spirit who is from God, that we might understand the things freely given us by God. And we impart this in words not taught by human wisdom but taught by the Spirit, interpreting spiritual truths to

those who are spiritual. The natural person does not accept the things of the Spirit of God, for they are folly to him, and he is not able to understand them because they are spiritually discerned. The spiritual person judges all things, but is himself to be judged by no one. "For who has understood the mind of the Lord so as to instruct him?" But we have the mind of Christ. (2:12–16)

What we see at work in the church at Corinth is one of those great mysteries or paradoxes of Christian existence. On the one hand, the Corinthians are believers, new creatures through baptism and faith. Despite his sharp criticisms, Paul can say to them, "Do you not know that you are God's temple and that God's Spirit dwells in you?" (3:16). And later, "your body is a temple of the Holy Spirit within you" (6:19). Whatever they are doing wrong, they remain the temple of the Holy Spirit. And yet, their individual and collective behavior testifies to just the opposite. They are still only "natural," operating according to the old sinful model.

It's imperative to keep this paradox in mind as we work through the longest biblical discussion of the charismata in I Corinthians 12 through 14. The Corinthians do, indisputably, have and exercise the charismatic gifts—as Paul has said right at the opening of his letter. But all too often these immature Christians have misused them. Paul doesn't deny that they really do have the Spirit and the attendant gifts, but he realizes that they haven't understood the charismata yet. They need better instruction. That's what these chapters are all about, beginning with 12:1: "Now concerning spiritual gifts [pneumatikōn], brothers, I do not want you to be uninformed."

The first principle Paul lays down—and one well attested by other New Testament writers (see, for example, John 14 to 17 and I John 4:1–3)—is that "no one speaking in the Spirit of God ever says 'Jesus is accursed!' and no one can say 'Jesus is Lord' except in the Holy Spirit" (12:3). So, first and foremost, the purpose of spiritual gifts is to draw people closer to Jesus Christ in faith and love.

Having established that, Paul moves on to the next point: there is only one Spirit, but there are many gifts. Every believer gets a gift from the Spirit, but not every believer gets every gift. The charismata are distributed according to God's good pleasure, not to please the individual persons receiving them but "for the common good" (12:7). Examples of these "manifestations of the Spirit" are the speaking of wisdom, the speaking of knowledge, faith, healing, working miracles, prophecy, the distinction between spirits, various kinds of tongues, and the interpretation of tongues. "All these are empowered by one and the same Spirit, who apportions to each one individually as he wills" (12:11).

From here, Paul moves into his famous body-and-members analogy of the church. It is a classic reflection on unity and diversity. Today it is applied to many aspects of church life, but it's imperative to remember that the immediate context for it was the exercise of charismata in Paul's churches and to counter spiritual elitism. Christian unity is anchored in the fact that "in one Spirit we were all baptized into one body" (12:13). That is what makes it irrelevant whether you are a Jew or a Greek or of any other nation, whether you are a slave or a free person or in any other socioeconomic condition, whether you are male or female. God puts all these people together to make the one body of Christ (cf. Gal 3:27–29). The ultimate goal is that "there may be no division in the body, but that the members may have the same care for one another. If one member suffers, all suffer together; if one member is honored, all rejoice together" (12:25–26). Paul summarizes in conclusion: "Now you are the body of Christ and individually members of it" (12:27).

Once he has clarified the nature of the body of Christ, Paul can get back to the more specific topic of the charismata and the right way to exercise them within the body. God, he says, has given to the church "first apostles, second prophets, third teachers, then miracles, then gifts of healing, helping, administrating, and various kinds of tongues" (12:28). He then asks whether everyone is or does every one of these things—the obvious answer being no, they do not. Nevertheless, he recommends that the Corinthians "earnestly desire the higher gifts" (12:31).

At this point Paul introduces a new topic, his famous chapter 13 on divine love or *agapē*. Again, while this passage is famous and used in many different contexts, especially at weddings, it's important to remember why Paul brings it up here: it's part of his discussion of the charismata. Yes, we are all one body, and yes, we each have our own Spirit-appointed gifts for the body. But our life together and our spiritual powers are for the purpose of participating in divine love. Paul esteems the charismata very highly—after all, he has just encouraged the Corinthians earnestly to desire the higher gifts—and yet he can say, "If I speak in the tongues of men and of angels, but have not love, I am a noisy gong or a clanging cymbal. And if I have prophetic powers, and understand all mysteries and all knowledge, and if I have all faith, so as to remove mountains, but have not love, I am nothing" (13:1–2). Prophecies, tongues, and knowledge will pass away, but love will endure forever. Love is *never* called a charisma. It is universal, not a gift for certain people only.

Christians who belong to churches that do not cultivate the charismata usually take this to be the end of the discussion. Love is better than everything else, and the charismata will cease anyway, so why bother to seek tongues and prophecies? But it is extremely important to keep going and not stop at chapter 13. For Paul does not pit the one against the other. Chapter 14 begins: "Pursue love, and earnestly desire the spiritual gifts, especially that you may prophesy" (14:1). Love and the charismata should go together.

As far as the charismata go, however, Paul has his distinct preferences. Prophecy is better than tongues, since the former is in language that everyone can understand but tongues are intelligible to no one but God. (Notice that Paul assumes tongues to be only glossolalia, not xenolalia.) Prophecy is usually assumed nowadays to mean the prediction of future events, which is certainly a possibility—the prophet Agabus predicted a famine in Acts 11—but Paul remarks here that "the one who prophesies speaks to people for their upbuilding and encouragement and consolation" (14:3). In other words, telling the future is not the main thing Paul has in mind when he speaks about prophecy. Prophecy benefits the whole church, while tongues benefit only the individual (and then only the individual's spirit, not the individual's mind), unless there is interpretation.

Nevertheless, in case the Corinthians got the wrong idea that Paul was simply opposed to tongues, he adds, "Now I want you all to speak in tongues, but even more to prophesy" (14:5). The issue is what to do with the believers' enthusiasm for the charismata. Spiritual gifts should not be only or primarily beneficial on a personal level, but good for the whole community. "So with yourselves, since you are eager for manifestations of the Spirit, strive to excel in building up the church" (14:12). And not just the already-existing church, Paul clarifies, but also those on the outside who may be convicted by the truth of the prophecy and so come to faith. By contrast, hearing tongues might just convince unbelievers that Christians are out of their minds! Paul gives his own personal perspective: "I thank God that I speak in tongues more than all of you. Nevertheless, in church I would rather speak five words with my mind in order to instruct others, than ten thousand words in a tongue" (14:18–19).

He concludes his discussion of charismata with guidelines for the church's worship.

When you come together, each one has a hymn, a lesson, a revelation, a tongue, or an interpretation. Let all things be done for building up. If any speak in a tongue, let there be only two or at most three, and each in turn, and let someone interpret. But if there is no one to interpret, let each of them keep silent in church and speak to himself and to God. Let two or three prophets speak, and let the others weigh what is said. If a revelation is made to another sitting there, let the first be silent. For you can all prophesy one by one, so that all may learn and all be encouraged, and the spirits of prophets are subject to prophets. For God is not a God of confusion but of peace. (14:26–33)

A few details are worth noting here. First, Paul assumes that *everyone* will have something to contribute to the worship service. Public speech is not restricted only to a few. Second, whatever happens should be edifying to all. It's acceptable to have speaking in tongues, but it's best to limit it to two or three people, one at a time, with interpretation. If there is no interpretation, it is better for the tongues-speakers to keep silent. Prophets are also allowed to speak, two or three at most, but they are not to pass judgment on their own prophecies. Others are to weigh or judge what is said. Taking turns is essential, as is learning to keep quiet when it's not your time to speak. Paul does not accept the idea that the Spirit overcomes people with such force that they can't keep quiet. "The spirits of prophets are subject to prophets"—and after all God is for peace, not confusion. Worship is most definitely to be communal and participatory, but it is not to be wild, disorderly, or rambunctious. Paul's final judgment on the matter is that the Corinthians should "earnestly desire to prophesy, and do not forbid speaking in tongues. But all things should be done decently and in order" (14:39–40).

Evidently, the possession of charismata didn't mean that the Corinthians were particularly good at using them! They required quite a lot of instruction in order even to begin using them for the right purpose and with the right attitude. "Brothers, do not be children in your thinking. Be infants in evil, but in your thinking be mature" (14:20).

Having now reviewed Paul's in-depth discussion of the charismata, we can work through a number of contemporary questions to explore what the experience of the first-century church in Corinth might have to say to us today. The first question likely to arise is: but are the charismata really real?

Yes, as far as the biblical writers are concerned. The charismata are real. They are not illusions or self-deception. They are gifts from God. They are also normal. It is nothing unusual or exceptional for a church to have these gifts and in great abundance. And there is no suggestion that they are only temporary phenomena in the history of the church, meant to pass away within the first few decades after Jesus' resurrection. (Some have made this argument to explain the absence of the charismata in so many churches; we will take it up in more detail in the chapter on history.)

Even this modest claim poses a problem for most Christians who do not practice or have not witnessed charismata. For many, the chief difficulty is that the charismata are "supernatural." On reflection, this objection is an odd one coming from people who believe in the incarnation, resurrection, and ascension of Jesus Christ and his real physical presence at the Lord's Supper! Perhaps these matters are easier to accept because they concern the one whom we know to be God, but making "supernatural" claims for mere human beings is a much more troubling claim.

Several things can be said to these legitimate concerns. First of all, while the Scriptures do assert a very strong distinction between Creator and creature, they do not accept the distinction between "supernatural" and "natural." In fact, the very belief in creation by a Creator undoes that distinction. All things come from God, although they are not themselves God; all things have a "supernatural" origin. It is not a mistake when we call a newborn baby or a beautiful sunrise a "miracle." One of the effects of faith is to see the miraculous hand of God in all things, even those we might have assumed to be merely "natural"—which in this case would mean "independent of God." But the Bible teaches that nothing exists independently of God. "In [God] we live and move and have our being" (Acts 17:28); "in [Christ] all things hold together" (Col 1:17). The problem then is not that charismata are supernatural, but rather that we do not perceive *everything* as "supernatural." Many Lutherans will accept charismata from Paul's list like helping, administration, and teaching because they seem to be "natural" and unspectacular. In truth, they should be considered as "supernatural" and divinely-given as all the others.

Likewise, there is a certain bias that assumes anything *really* "supernatural" must be utterly and absolutely different from what is "natural." Thus, if it seems like a charisma bears some continuity with a person's own "natural" endowments, it can't really be divine in origin. But again, this distinction fails from a biblical perspective. All of our endowments are

God-given gifts. Those who find themselves to have a natural talent for music, or organization, or athletics did nothing to earn that talent. They can certainly develop and strengthen it, but they experience it first of all as a gift. This reality is felt even more strongly by those who *wish* they had a gift for something and discover that, in sad reality, they don't. The gift was not given to them. Thus there is nothing contradictory in a Spirit-given charisma making use of and enhancing the "natural" endowments in a person, for the latter are every bit as much a divine gift as the former.

However, more problematic for Christians outside the Pentecostal fold is what they see as a tendency to abuse charismatic powers. It is unfortunately all too common for earnest religious people to get burned by the deceptions of charlatans and false prophets. Even worse than this is the abuse perpetrated by people who really do have spiritual gifts but employ them for evil purposes.

But there is a difference between rejecting a particular alleged miracle or charisma on evidence, and rejecting all possible miracles and charismata on principle. Many people have suffered from dishonest claims about spiritual phenomena and have therefore concluded that they don't actually occur at all. This is understandable, but it is important from a theological perspective to separate the issues of use and misuse. As already noted, the Scriptures testify to charismata and miracles as ordinary events in the church. But the Scriptures are also extremely well aware of the problem of false prophets and teachers, of the need for discernment in every case of spiritual gifts, and of the imperative of teaching people what their gifts mean and how to use them rightly.

Jesus issues many warnings against false prophets in Matthew's Gospel. "Beware of false prophets, who come to you in sheep's clothing but inwardly are ravenous wolves" (7:15). "And many false prophets will arise and lead many astray" (24:11). "For false christs and false prophets will arise and perform great signs and wonders, so as to lead astray, if possible, even the elect" (24:24). This last verse conveys an extremely alarming piece of information: false prophets can perform convincing miracles. Moses had experienced the same problem with Pharaoh's magicians in Egypt. II Thessalonians 2:9 knows of the problem, too: "The coming of the lawless one is by the activity of Satan with all power and false signs and wonders." All these verses lead us to an important rule of discernment: the Christian recognition of spiritual gifts is *not* the same thing as worshipping power.

Power can be employed by the wicked and the enemies of God. A "miracle" on its own should not convince anyone.

The Epistles give us more detailed information on discerning the spirits. For example, it is written in II Peter 2:1–3a, "But false prophets also arose among the people, just as there will be false teachers among you, who will secretly bring in destructive heresies, even denying the Master who bought them, bringing upon themselves swift destruction. And many will follow their sensuality, and because of them the way of truth will be blasphemed. And in their greed they will exploit you with false words." A false prophet will be exposed by his false teaching and immoral behavior. And if that isn't enough, a false prophet will inevitably be motivated by financial gain. This is an unfortunately very common deception perpetrated on trusting Christians, who are fooled into giving beyond their means to support someone who claims to have a divine mandate. Any prophet claiming to need huge amounts of money—especially one who will not show you his accounting books—should be tested carefully before any donations are made and before any miracles are believed.

I John 4 also takes up the discernment question. The apostle writes, "Beloved, do not believe every spirit, but test the spirits to see whether they are from God, for many false prophets have gone out into the world. By this you know the Spirit of God: every spirit that confesses that Jesus Christ has come in the flesh is from God, and every spirit that does not confess Jesus is not from God" (vv. 1–3a). Like II Peter, this Epistle connects false teaching with spirits that are in conflict with the Spirit of God. The rule is that a trustworthy spirit will confess Jesus Christ as Lord—much as Paul said in I Corinthians. Of course, it is also possible that a false prophet or a charlatan will have read this in the Bible and therefore pay lip service to Christ while exploiting his people. It will require wise pastoral care and careful theological discernment to protect Christians from such abusers of the good name of Jesus, as Paul did in confronting the false prophet Elymas in Cyprus (Acts 13).

It's worth mentioning that Pentecostals and their forebears were perfectly well aware of the dangers on this score, too. Seth Cook Rees, a participant in the nineteenth-century American healing movement, wrote in 1897: "There is probably not a man in all our prisons who was placed there for counterfeiting the copper cent. So the devil counterfeits only the good, God-sent and God-ordained things, and the more valuable the genuine the more elaborate and labored his imitation. Let us not reject the gold because there is some brass in circulation."[1]

False prophets represent an extreme abuse. But what about troubles in the ordinary operation of charismata in a Christian congregation, as the Corinthians bear ample witness to?

Here again, non-Pentecostals are likely to react with alarm above all. Lots of terrible scenarios spring to mind: a person who claims to have prophetic powers will start ordering others around; a person of questionable character will suddenly gain great moral authority because she speaks in tongues; people who don't speak in tongues will be considered less spiritual or mature than those who do; fights will break out between one faction of the congregation that welcomes the charismata and the other that doesn't. Worship itself will be constantly interrupted by explosions of apparent prophecies and incomprehensible tongues. It may well seem that the charismata are more trouble than they're worth!

Once again, these concerns are real and legitimate. Many Pentecostal Christians admit to the decidedly unspiritual infighting and divisions that mar their communities. The charismata are no guarantee of a smooth and peaceful existence. Power, though necessary for doing any good at all, always attracts evil and those who would like to exploit it for evil purposes. This applies just as much, though, to bureaucracies and hierarchies and other forms of power in the church that make no use of the charismata. The Scriptures offer us no solution other than turning again and again to God and doing the hard work of discernment.

What we learned in I Corinthians helps sort through these problems. As Paul says right at the outset of the letter, "you are not lacking in any gift," and yet he immediately launches into an attack on them for being such utterly unspiritual people! In other words, *reception of a spiritual gift does not automatically make you into a spiritual person*. You can receive the gift and still live in the "flesh," still be controlled by sin, still indulge in vice and unrighteousness. God does not give a charisma in order to say, "This person is better than everyone else." Rather, God gives charismata in order for people to learn to use them rightly for the good of the whole church. It is a risky business—but a risk that God is apparently willing to take.

If anything, God's granting of charismata mirrors the structure of salvation itself. The Father sent His Son while we were still enemies (Rom

---

1. Quoted in Dayton, *The Theological Roots of Pentecostalism*, 135.

5:10), while we were still dead in our trespasses (Eph 2:5), as a free gift for us and for our salvation. Just because He has offered us salvation does not mean that all of us will accept it. Even those of us who do accept it will not always respond properly, joyfully, or obediently. Here we draw close to the heart of Lutheran teaching: God gives first, *before* there is any change or response on your part. God gives *in order to* change you. He does not demand the change first or as a condition of the gift. The gift is categorical and unconditional. And it is the same with the charismata. You do nothing to earn them; they are free gifts, graced-things. But the possibility remains that you might abuse the gifts given to you.

Another real danger is that the charismata may divide the community instead of drawing it closer together. Remember, it is exactly in the context of spiritual gifts that Paul presents his famous analogy of the church as a body. One member might think that her gift is all-sufficient and the others less valuable, while another might suffer from terrible envy that someone else was given a gift that he wanted and was denied. Pride and envy are well-documented sins throughout the Scripture. They led to the terrible betrayal of proud Joseph by his envious brothers in the book of Genesis.

Here again Paul turns worldly wisdom upside down. "The parts of the body that seem to be weaker are indispensable, and on those parts of the body that we think less honorable we bestow the greater honor, and our unpresentable parts are treated with greater modesty, which our more presentable parts do not require. But God has so composed the body, giving greater honor to the part that lacked it, that there may be no division in the body" (I Corinthians 12:22–25). Neither the proud nor the envious are justified in their attitudes. Someone who prophecies has no right to look down on someone who "only" has the gift of administration, and likewise the one with the gift of helping should not feel inferior to or jealous of the one who speaks in tongues. Every gift is truly a gift, to the person and to the body as a whole, and all deserve recognition and honor. Here again, wise pastoral care will have to cope with these negative emotions as they arise and to help those suffering from them to grow into greater spiritual maturity.

Yet another concern is the disruptive nature of charismata. Some people have experienced and some simply fear that the liturgy will be taken over by odd noises, strange behavior, and unpredictable outbursts. Paul was well aware of this. It would have been the common experience of those who participated in the Hellenistic religions of the world around him. In those cults, worshippers expected total possession of their being by the "god" or "spirit," with a temporary erasure of their own personality.

But the Holy Spirit does not work like that. Paul makes a point of saying that the prophet has control of the prophecies. Tongues do not need to come bursting out. It's entirely respectable and appropriate to limit their expression to two or at most three per service, and maybe even less if there is no interpretation (which seems to be fairly typical, according to the reports of many Pentecostals). Tongues can even be kept for private devotions, though if they contribute to the upbuilding of the congregation then they can be given a place. For this reason, it's quite common in Pentecostal worship to play instrumental music at a certain point in the service, allowing everyone to speak in tongues at once to praise God without disruption of the liturgy.

Finally, there is the worry that charismatic experiences will usurp the Scripture as the norm of the Christian faith. As we have had cause to note earlier in this book, Pentecostals from the beginning have been aware of that danger and guarded against it. For instance, there was an early case of someone attempting to "write in tongues." The community prayed about it and ultimately ruled it out, since there was no scriptural precedent. Of course, in any given congregation, there is the danger of charismatic "revelations" carrying more weight than Scripture—but again, that can just as easily happen with "secular" or other "ordinary" notions that take root in the church. The one is not more dangerous than the other. Christians are always called upon to be vigilant in their practice of the faith.

But this rule does assume that tongues and other charismata are happening at all. It has probably been the more common experience for most Lutherans to have read the relevant chapters of I Corinthians but more or less ignored them, except for the part about love, because it all seemed so distant from ordinary church experience. Tongues were apparently something that was a big deal long ago, but they're not part of church life now. We definitely pray for the sick, but we don't look or pray for miraculous acts of healing. We automatically distrust anyone who prophesies, at least in a spontaneous way; the word is nowadays reserved for someone who critiques social and political abuses, somewhat like the way the Old Testament prophets did.

Thus, there is a troubling disconnect when Lutherans encounter Pentecostals who claim that the charismata are entirely normal parts of *their* church life. A common response might be sheer skepticism: the

Pentecostals are deluded. Certainly plenty of other Christians and the news media thought so at the time of the Azusa Street revival. Another response might be confusion about God's purposes. If these things are so important for the upbuilding of the church, why did they disappear for centuries, if not a millennium or more? Another reaction might be anxiety. Has my own church betrayed me by keeping the charismata secret or not paying more attention to them? Is my Christian life empty and worthless because it doesn't include them? Much of the Lutheran reaction to charismata will depend on the Pentecostals they meet. Some will be warm, wise, open-hearted, and open-minded. Others will be greedy, cruel, controlling, and ignorant. (One could say the same about Lutherans.) It is impossible to give a universally applicable answer. Discernment is required in every case.

But building on what we have learned in this chapter, a few things can be said. The first is that the Spirit is given to every believer (I Cor 12:6, 7, 11, 13). You cannot be a believer without the Spirit! "*I believe* that by my own understanding or strength *I cannot believe* in Jesus Christ my Lord or come to him, but instead *the Holy Spirit has called me* through the gospel, enlightened me with his gifts, made me holy and kept me in the true faith, just as he calls, gathers, enlightens, and makes holy the whole Christian church on earth."[2] So said Luther in his Small Catechism on the Third Article of the Creed. Lack of charismata in any obvious form does not mean lack of the Holy Spirit.

Second, God distributes the gifts as He sees fit. The gifts that a particular Christian or congregation have may not look much like those commonly cultivated by Pentecostals, but they are still gifts. It is essential to welcome and value everything God gives and not be weighed down by envy or filled with pride. "What do you have that you did not receive? If then you received it, why do you boast as if you did not receive it?" (I Cor 4:7).

Third, note how often Paul has to encourage the Corinthians to desire the spiritual gifts, prophecy in particular. In other words, he assumes that they will forget or neglect the charismata without his encouragement. The same theme appears elsewhere in the New Testament. "You do not have, because you do not ask" (Jas 4:2). "If you then, who are evil, know how to give good gifts to your children, how much more will the heavenly Father give the Holy Spirit to those who ask him!" (Luke 11:13). God does not necessarily impose the charismata on His people. He seems to prefer it when they actively desire and ask for the spiritual gifts. However, the charismata

---

2. Luther, "The Small Catechism," in *The Book of Concord*, 355.

are not to be desired for their own sake. They are a way of drawing nearer to Christ the Lord and building up the whole church. They are certainly not for spiritual self-aggrandizement.

Another thing to notice is that the charismata appear to be given in the context of the church's common worship or as a direct outgrowth of it. While some Pentecostals have had charismata come upon them while alone or independently of any other experience, the majority of them testify to receiving the charismata during or as a result of worship and prayer with other Christians. So it stands to reason that a church or congregation that never seeks charismata *together* is very unlikely to see them at all.

On the other hand, it's quite possible that the charismata of the more unusual type do actually exist among Lutherans but are kept hidden for fear of disapproval. If you start asking with an open heart and non-judgmental attitude, you might well find that there are many quiet "charismatics" in your midst who have never had the necessary teaching or encouragement to make better use of their gifts. Paul would encourage us to make these gifts public and put them to good use. "Having gifts [*charismata*] that differ according to the grace [*charin*] given to us, let us use them: if prophecy, in proportion to our faith; if service, in our serving; the one who teaches, in his teaching; the one who exhorts, in his exhortation; the one who contributes, in generosity; the one who leads, with zeal; the one who does acts of mercy, with cheerfulness" (Rom 12:4–8).

Scripture shows that there is always room for more of God: more gifts, more depth of understanding, more breadth of love. "Be filled with the Spirit" (Eph 5:18b)—or, more accurately, "Keep on being filled with the Spirit." It is not greed to ask for more. Asking greedily would not procure the desired result anyway. In any event, God remains the giver and gives as He sees fit. The "more" is up to Him. But He commands and exhorts us to ask. Ask and seek for all the gifts; gratefully receive what you are given; honor what is given to others; always test the spirits.

One final word should be said before moving on to the next topic. When Scripture paints us a picture of the gifts that come from God, there is always one essential element in the mix: the cross. There is no Jesus the Messiah—healer of illnesses, exorcist of demons, preacher with authority, feeder of thousands—without the crucifixion. It is the cup given him to drink, and he cannot turn aside from it. In analogous fashion, Paul the mighty apostle, preacher, and evangelist is given a thorn in his flesh for the very purpose of preventing him from being too elated by all the other glorious gifts he has received. Both of these New Testament examples draw upon consistent Old Testament themes: Jacob wins God's blessing but at the price of an injured hip, Jeremiah the prophet suffers ostracism and imprisonment, the Suffering Servant exercises the gift of healing but at the cost of his own chastisement and wounds. The charismata are not given to guarantee a happy, pain-free, victorious life. They are given for the sake of faith and are to be exercised faithfully. For Christians, faith always includes bearing the cross.

For Further Reading

John Koenig, *Charismata: God's Gifts for God's People* (Philadelphia: Westminster, 1978). Koenig, a Lutheran pastor who later became an Episcopal priest, wrote this study while still Lutheran and encountering the Charismatic renewal among American Lutherans and other Christians. It is a careful exploration of all the biblical teaching on gifts and charismata and very highly recommended.

Arnold Bittlinger, *Gifts and Ministries* (Grand Rapids: Eerdmans, 1973), is a selection of writings by a prominent Lutheran Charismatic in the German-speaking world. The German original is *Charisma und Amt* (Calw: Calwer Verlag, 1967).

CHAPTER 7

History

THE SCRIPTURE DISCUSSES THINGS like tongues, prophecy, and healing, but the plain fact is that they were not common, obvious, or everyday parts of church life for 1800 or more years of its history. This was and remains the biggest obstacle to accepting the Pentecostal movement and its offshoots nowadays. Thus, defending the reappearance of the charismata (or, on the opposite side, disproving their alleged reappearance) has been a major preoccupation of the intra-ecclesial battles. Coupled with a potent eschatology—that is to say, awaiting the imminent return of Jesus in glory—a particular theory or philosophy of church history has become an essential aspect of Pentecostal theology.

Though most of them have not been intended to explain the loss of charismatic gifts, many other theories of church history have also grown and developed throughout the course of church history. The need for such a theory seems to grow more urgent as church history stretches on longer and longer after the ascension. The New Testament itself reflects a shift from the expectation of Jesus' immediate return to a sense that maybe other things need to happen first. Luke-Acts certainly takes the latter option, with its vivid depiction of the spread of the gospel throughout the world. Paul undergoes the biggest shift, from his Thessalonian correspondence announcing the Parousia within his lifetime (e.g. I Thess 4:13–18) to his letter to the Romans explaining that a delayed return and Jewish unbelief are for the sake of the ingrafting of the nations (chs. 9–11). The two Epistles of Peter explicitly address the delayed return of Christ in the context of the church's suffering. They ultimately conclude that "with the Lord one day is as a thousand years, and a thousand years as one day. The Lord is not slow to fulfill his promise as some count slowness, but is patient toward you, not wishing that any should perish, but that all should reach repentance" (II Pet 3:8b–9).

The earliest church fathers tended toward chiliasm, from the Greek word *chilia* ("thousand"), which, drawing on Revelation 20, anticipates that Christ will return in glory and then reign for a thousand years with the saints. Already by Augustine's time, though, belief in chiliasm began to fade. It was only later in the Middle Ages that slicing up human history in general, and church history in particular, became a special fascination. Joachim of Fiore, a twelfth-century Italian mystic, theorized a division of history into three epochs, based on Revelation 14: that of the Father, from creation to Christ; that of the Son, from the incarnation till the year 1260 AD; and that of the Spirit, which Joachim supposed would commence shortly. In the age of the Spirit, all flesh would know God and the kingdom would be fully established on earth. As has been the case with all predictions of impending epochs or the end of time, Joachim was proven wrong.

This did not discourage future efforts, however. The reformers saw the world going up in flames about them, with political upheavals and various sects reducing both civil and ecclesial society to chaos. At first they feared that the end might be drawing near. In time, though, they pulled back from such extreme views and invested themselves instead in building long-term institutions for the good of the earth and human society, such as schools and community care for the poor. Indeed, their urgency stemmed not from fear of the end of the world but fear of not making good use of the gospel while it dwelt among them. As Luther wrote in the context of urging city leaders to open schools:

> Germany, I am sure, has never before heard so much of God's word as it is hearing today; certainly we read nothing of it in history. If we let it just slip by without thanks and honor, I fear we shall suffer a still more dreadful darkness and plague. O my beloved Germans, buy while the market is at your door; gather in the harvest while there is sunshine and fair weather; make use of God's grace and word while it is there! For you should know that God's word and grace is like a passing shower of rain which does not return where it has once been. It has been with the Jews, but when it's gone it's gone, and now they have nothing. Paul brought it to the Greeks; but again when it's gone it's gone, and now they have the Turk. Rome and the Latins also had it; but when it's gone it's gone, and now they have the pope. And you Germans need not think that you will have it forever, for ingratitude and contempt

will not make it stay. Therefore, seize it and hold it fast, whoever can; for lazy hands are bound to have a lean year.[1]

As the foregoing shows, the reformers had their own take on the meaning of church history. A consistent theme of Luther and Melanchthon in the Confessional writings is how their evangelical teaching is, in fact, more faithful to the Bible and the early church than the recent Roman aberrations. This view implies that it is possible for the church to get off track, and that God will need to intervene to set things right—itself a theory of church history's twists and turns. The reformers saw the need to right the wrongs of the church of their time, but overall they expressed confidence in God's guiding hand throughout the church's history.

Later Lutherans varied widely in their response. Matthias Flacius, a second-generation Lutheran, was the editor of an enormous history of the church known as the *Magdeburg Centuries*, the first church history to be based entirely on primary sources. Its express purpose was to demonstrate the underlying continuity of Christian doctrine from the apostolic times to the present while also showing the ways in which the church—the Roman church in particular—had introduced error. Pietists, for their part, were optimistic about human potential, shifting their theological emphasis from justification to sanctification. An example of this is a 1693 work by Philipp Spener, founding father of Pietism: "Assertion of Hope for Future Better Times" (*Behauptung der Hoffnung künfftiger Besserer Zeiten*). A later Pietist, Johann Albrecht Bengel, published a couple of works speculating about the end times, which enjoyed immense popularity. As time went on and Protestant Christianity became the uncontested norm in certain countries, some figures in the church became so affirming of the world that the status quo itself was quietly blessed. In such circles, there was never any need to think about the final judgment. Lutheran philosopher Søren Kierkegaard is the most famous critic of such bourgeois religiosity.

Overall, Protestants avoided end-time speculation for the first several centuries of their existence. (The exceptions were certain Anabaptists, Huguenots, and Puritans, but they usually remained on the margins even of Christian society.) Perhaps Protestants had learned their lesson, since the end did not actually come in the sixteenth century despite their identification of the pope with the Antichrist. Catholics of the same period offered their own theories of Revelation and history to oppose the Protestant equation of pope with Antichrist. They drew up detailed plans of how history

1. Martin Luther, "To the Councilmen of All Cities," in *Luther's Works*, 45:352–53.

would unfold at the end. Such Catholic interest in the various supposed epochs of church history did much to deter further Protestant interest.

That is, until the early nineteenth century, when divisions of history and the end times came back in vogue due to the efforts of John Nelson Darby (1800–1882). Darby was one of the founding fathers of the Plymouth Brethren, a small Irish and English denomination that rejected existing church structures and attempted to recreate more authentic biblical ones. He basically invented modern Protestant dispensationalism: the belief that history is organized into successive dispensations in which different religious rules or realities govern. A tripartite dispensation has always been the most popular, slicing up history according to Father, Son, and Spirit. (This forgets one of the oldest principles of trinitarian theology, namely that all three Persons always work together in every action.) But there have also been sevenfold dispensations proposed to correspond to the seven days of creation. The most influential of these is found in the *Scofield Reference Bible* (1909, revised edition 1917), which has done more than any other book to sway Evangelical and Pentecostal Protestants toward dispensationalism and eschatological speculation. The fact that it overlapped with the destruction of nineteenth-century optimism during the First World War probably explains much of its popularity.

Dispensationalism usually goes hand in hand with premillennialism, which is basically a rerun of early-church chiliasm, anticipating a thousand-year reign of Christ on earth. Counter to premillennialism are postmillennialism, which expects that human beings themselves will establish a thousand-year reign of righteousness blessed by Christ from heaven, and amillennialism, which takes Revelation 20 to be figurative, not literal, language. The Lutheran Confessions forbid millennialist theories: Article XVII of the Augsburg Confession condemns the notion that "before the resurrection of the dead saints and righteous people alone will possess a secular kingdom and will annihilate all the ungodly."[2]

Prophecies of the end times and of massive historical upheavals captivated the Protestant imagination on a wide scale in the nineteenth century. Restorationist movements seeking to recreate the New Testament church sprang up as their leaders predicted the imminent end of history. New groups like the Seventh-Day Adventists and the Jehovah's Witnesses emerged in response to specific prophecies of the last day. Somehow

2. Melanchthon, "The Augsburg Confession," in *The Book of Concord*, 51, German text.

these groups managed to carry on even after the continuation of history proved them wrong, which non-event Adventists refer to as "The Great Disappointment."

Reading the signs and interpreting them against a larger scheme of history kept going strong into the twentieth century. For example, the creation of the modern nation of Israel in 1948, and the reappearance of distinctly Jewish Christianity in the Messianic Jewish movement of the 1960s, were both taken as proof that Paul's hope for the restoration of Israel was about to be fulfilled. "Wars and rumors of wars" were applied to current conflicts, of which there were many. Premillennialism also prophesied "the rapture," the notion that all the faithful would be taken directly up into heaven when the end comes, and "the tribulation," an extended period of intense suffering for the lukewarm and unfaithful left on the earth. These ideas got a fresh boost with *The Late, Great Planet Earth* by Hal Lindsey in 1970, and then again with the immensely popular "Left Behind" series of novels published in the 1990s and 2000s.

The early Pentecostals inherited many dispensationalist and premillennialist tendencies from the Plymouth Brethren, the *Scofield Reference Bible*, and the various Restoration movements. One scholar even asserts that "[t]he second coming of Jesus was the central concern of the initial Pentecostal message,"[3] even more so than tongues or Spirit baptism. The urgent expectation of Jesus' return—confessed as the "soon-coming king" in the Foursquare Gospel lingo—put eschatology front and center. However, it's important to realize that the vast majority of Pentecostals did not and do not indulge in predicting the exact date of Jesus' return in glory, as the aforementioned nineteenth-century movements did. They wait in hope but do not set an exact date and time.

A practical problem for the brand-new Pentecostals, however, was that many of their erstwhile allies in premillennial expectation rejected any possibility of the reestablishment of charismatic gifts. Charismata belong to a prior dispensation, the other premillennialists argued, so Pentecostals were wrong to claim them now in this later dispensation. Such a view is called "cessationism," referring to the fact that charismatic gifts have "ceased."

Even more formidable foes were Reformed theologians of a rigorous type, chief among them the American B. B. Warfield, who saw in Pentecostal claims nothing but the most diabolical form of fraud. He claimed the church fathers on his side. Augustine in the West and John Chrysostom

---

3. Faupel, *The Everlasting Gospel*, 20.

in the East had already noticed, and lamented, the loss of the charismatic gifts among their people. These two church fathers drew the conclusion that would persist for centuries to come: that the charismata were a special gift to the apostolic church but were never intended to continue once the church was well-established. Occasional later Christian writers, especially in monastic communities, would testify to powerful experiences of the Holy Spirit, and healings were not unknown, though they were likely to be linked to saints or their shrines. The reformers echoed Augustine in assuming that the charismata ended with the apostolic age.

The problem is a serious one. If indeed the Spirit gave these gifts so freely and abundantly, as Paul said in his letters, why exactly *had* they disappeared for so long? Why were they coming back now? Did it mean something special on the grand stage of history? If so, what? And how would we know?

Pentecostals were not slow to offer their own new theories of church history, accounting both for past spiritual dryness and the suddenness of their own arrival on the scene. For instance, T. B. Barratt, a Norwegian Methodist-turned-Pentecostal, published a treatise in 1909 entitled "In the Days of the Latter Rain." Here he argues that *"the old-time Apostolic power is returning back to believers"* and that they are being given back "the position by the first christians, that has been lost to a great extent during the darkness of bygone centuries."[4] This loss and restoration, said Barratt, had already been prophesied by Joel: "Be glad, O children of Zion, and rejoice in the Lord your God, for he has given the early rain for your vindication; he has poured down for you abundant rain, the early and the latter rain, as before" (2:23). What was happening in Barratt's day, he thought, was the latter rain, "the mighty outpouring of the Holy Ghost towards the close of this Dispensation." Barratt foresaw *"stupendous changes"* ahead for the human race and exhorted everyone to rejoice in them.[5]

However, even if people didn't rejoice, that wouldn't surprise Barratt, because that's how it has always happened—restoration angers the complacent. He invokes church history as proof of the pattern he sees repeating itself in the present. A restoration of lost Christian teaching came with Martin Luther, who is inevitably the first figure in the restoration of lost truth and

---

4. Barratt, *In the Days of the Latter Rain*, pp. 22, 24, his italics and upper/lowercase letters in all quotations. Barratt may have gotten the idea from preacher D. Wesley Myland at the Stone Church, who preached on the same theme earlier in the same year.

5. Barratt, *In the Days of the Latter Rain*, 24.

practice in Pentecostal histories. Luther "had to run the gauntlet of church hatred and the sneers of the world. But by the grace of God he conquered."[6] Next came John Wesley, restoring sanctification and divine healing. Wesley is almost always the second in Pentecostal schemes of restoration. Then follow assorted other teachers—these vary more widely—continuing all the way up to the restoration of Spirit baptism and tongues in the Pentecostal movement. Despite the constant resistance, Barratt maintains, there has always been a remnant throughout the whole history of the church that spoke in tongues and kept the true teaching of the early church alive. He assumes that most of the condemned heretics of the Middle Ages were the real Christians, persecuted and oppressed by the wealthy, established, formalistic, and spiritually dead church.

Not long after the appearance of Barratt's book, Aimee Semple McPherson (founder of the Foursquare Gospel Church) delivered a sermon with a similar theme, which later found its way into her book *This Is That* under the title "Lost and Restored: As I Saw It in My Vision." This time the historical account came with an image, as reproduced here:

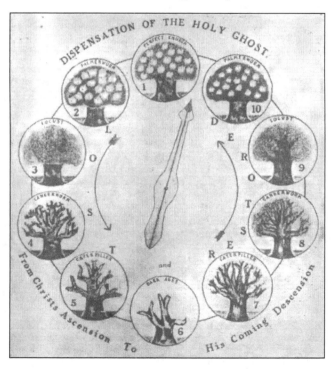

6. Barratt, *In the Days of the Latter Rain*, 25.

The title indicates McPherson's reliance on dispensationalist theory, opting for a trinitarian pattern. The difference here is that even within the third dispensation there are movements up and down, better and worse.

The details of McPherson's theory come from Joel, just like Barratt's. But instead of focusing on the early and latter rain, her approach depends instead on these two verses: "That which the palmerworm hath left hath the locust eaten; and that which the locust hath left hath the cankerworm eaten; and that which the cankerworm hath left hath the caterpillar eaten" (1:4) and "And I will restore to you the years that the locust hath eaten, the cankerworm, and the caterpillar, and the palmerworm, my great army which I sent among you" (2:25).[7] The church, McPherson argued, began well, fully endowed with the nine gifts of I Corinthians 14:37 (wisdom, knowledge, faith, healing, miracles, prophecy, discerning the spirits, tongues, and interpretation of tongues) and the nine fruits of Galatians 5:22 (love, joy, peace, gentleness, goodness, faith, meekness, temperance, longsuffering). McPherson goes on to explain that this period was followed by a successive destruction of the church by various pests or worms: a diminution of the gifts and fruits of the Spirit, then "formality and sectarianism" that quenched the reception of the Holy Spirit as a personally indwelling presence, then the toleration of immorality among Christians, and finally the Dark Ages, "when the Church lost sight of justification by Faith, lost sight of the atonement, the blood of Jesus, there was a total eclipse and the face of the Sun of Righteousness was obscured. . ."[8] She vividly describes Christians torturing themselves in pointless ways so as to earn their salvation.

However, declares McPherson, God was not content to leave things that way. Even as the respective worms destroyed His church, He announced through the prophets that He would restore all that was lost. And the restoration would happen in the reverse order of its loss. So, as justification by faith was the last thing to be lost, it was also the first thing to be restored. At this point McPherson gives a colorful if inaccurate portrait of the Reformation:

> Martin Luther one day was walking up the steps of the cathedral on his hands and knees over broken glass, endeavoring to do penance, thereby seeking to atone for his sins. As he was toiling painfully and laboriously up the steps in this manner, blood trickling

---

7. Both verses here are taken from the 1611 King James Version of the Bible, which was still the main English translation in use in McPherson's day.

8. McPherson, *This Is That*, 393–94.

from his hands and knees, cut by the broken glass, he heard a voice from heaven saying: "Martin Luther, the Just shall live by Faith." At the words, a great light fell from Heaven. It banished the darkness and doubts, it illuminated the soul of Martin Luther, and revealed the finished work of Calvary and the blood that alone can atone for sin. . . The days that followed were eventful days, epoch-making days, fraught with self-sacrifice and suffering. The Lord had spoken, and promised that all the years that had been eaten should be restored, and out of the seas of travail and suffering that followed the preaching of Justification by Faith there was born a little body of blood-washed, fire-tried pilgrims, willing to suffer persecution for His Name's sake. You have read, perhaps, how Martin Luther and his followers were turned out of the churches, spoken against falsely, and accused of all manner of evil. As Martin Luther, Calvin, Knox [a Scottish Reformed minister], Fletcher [a trinitarian-dispensationalist Methodist preacher] and many other blessed children of the Lord, stood firm for the truths of salvation and a sinless life, they suffered all manner of persecution. . .[9]

A graphic description of martyrdoms at the hands of church authorities ensues. The history unfolds further with Wesley restoring sanctification and George Booth establishing the Salvation Army. The story culminates with the recent Pentecostal revivals around the world, the final evidence of God's intention to restore all that was lost. Clearly, from McPherson's perspective, it was an exciting time to be alive! The gifts and fruits of the Spirit were growing on the tree once more, and that meant Jesus would be coming soon.

Accounts of history as seen in Barratt or McPherson soon became standard doctrine for the nascent Pentecostal churches. A statement of faith from the Pentecostal Fellowship of North America asserted:

During the Reformation God used Martin Luther and others to restore to the world the doctrine of justification by faith. Rom. 5:1. Later on the Lord used the Wesleys and others in the great holiness movement to restore the gospel of sanctification by faith. Acts 26:18. Later still he used various ones to restore the gospel of Divine healing by faith (Jas. 5:14, 15), and the gospel of Jesus' second coming. Acts 1:11. Now the Lord is using many witnesses in the great Pentecostal movement to restore the gospel of the baptism with the Holy Ghost and fire (Luke 3:16; Acts 1:5) with signs

9. McPherson, *This Is That*, 395–6.

following. Mark 16:17, 18; Acts 2:4; 10:44–46; 19:6; 1:1–28:31. Thank God, we now have preachers of the whole gospel.[10]

Note the emphasis on Acts—the last citation is the entire book! History was coming around again as the New Testament church was returning to the present day. Pentecostals reasoned that if God is unchangeable, then His plan for the church would be unchangeable, too. The church in later times should always look like it did back at the beginning. If the church departed from the standard of its early years, then that could only be the work of the palmerworm and the cankerworm. If the church began to take on New Testament characteristics again, then it must be a new epoch in God's dealings with His people, heralding a fresh start.

The wildfire success of Pentecostalism seemed to confirm these theories of history. Within just a few years the movement had reached over fifty countries. Growth was initially slow in most places, and persecution from other Christians intense. But if your theory of history assumes a remnant-sized church and takes oppression for granted, then that is no cause for alarm but rather rejoicing.

Theories of history are hard to argue with. Every history, from the secular to the sacred, singles out certain events from the totality of everything that has happened. The events are strung together to assert a particular narrative headed in a certain direction. Who is to say which assemblage of events is "right" and which is "wrong"? Scientific method cannot conduct a double-blind study on human history!

Moreover, Pentecostal theories often assume that those who are involved in one stage of restoration will reject the next stage. Thus, the more people disagree with a particular theory of history's current phase, the more likely it is to be true. It is a self-authenticating position, repelling all challenges.

Yet it is difficult to sustain the early Pentecostals' level of eschatological fervor—as, in fact, the apostolic church discovered long ago. Once it becomes clear or at least seems plausible that Jesus is *not*, in fact, going to return any minute now, new considerations come to the fore. The excitement of being alive at such an important moment in history begins to fade. Revivals year after year become routine. Attendance dwindles. Organization and even the much-abhorred institutionalization become necessary. A new generation that has grown up in a very different set of circumstances has to be addressed (the second-generation challenge again!).

10. Quoted in Dayton, *The Theological Roots of Pentecostalism*, 19–20.

By the late 1930s, many American Pentecostals felt that they had lost the old passion of the early days of the movement. There was a slight uptick in activity in the 1940s with another series of revivals that started from an orphanage in Saskatchewan, Canada. It gave renewed hope and prompted another rewriting of history: now the early twentieth-century revival was labeled the early rain and the 1940s revival was seen to be the latter rain. Critically, though, at the very same time, America's Evangelicals and Fundamentalists were finally willing to make friends with Pentecostals. Pentecostals, grateful for respect at last, began to adapt themselves to the respectability demanded by their new allies. More and more Pentecostals were coming from the middle classes (at least in America and Europe), so the image of being a movement by and for the poor began to diminish. Meanwhile, other decline-and-restoration narratives arose in other segments of the church that were decidedly not Pentecostal: Walter Rauschenbusch created one to defend his Social Gospel, and liberation theologians created another to critique the Constantinian establishment of the church to the disadvantage of the poor.

The truly explosive growth of Pentecostal, Charismatic, and Neo-charismatic movements in the later twentieth century would seem to have brought the eschatological fervor back front and center. But there is generally less of a feeling that the return of Christ could happen any day now. In fact, some Neocharismatics have made the case that the kingdom has *already* come with power—which is why healings, prophecies, and tongues are possible at all. Meanwhile, a minority of Pentecostals have come to see ecumenism positively as a sign of the imminent second coming of Christ, since it is concerned with the unity of the church. This is an especially surprising development, as until very recently Pentecostals and Evangelicals tended to view the ecumenical movement with extreme suspicion.

It is worth noting that while all of this eschatological expectation was gripping Pentecostals throughout the twentieth century, a parallel though much calmer revolution was happening in biblical research. Critical scholars came to realize how important the genre of apocalyptic was for understanding the texts of the New Testament. Eschatology became a central theme of study once more and has stayed the course in biblical studies. While these scholars have generally belonged to historic or mainline churches that are decidedly not open to Pentecostal proposals, nevertheless it is striking that they have come to similar appreciations of the importance of this theme in the Bible. The critical difference is that mainline biblical scholars have been much less likely to appropriate apocalyptic thought forms for the church of today.

Whose version of church history is right?

Two things should be clear by now. One is that all Christians have a narrative or theory of church history. We all need to understand what God has been doing since He sent the Messiah and since He stopped sending the kinds of prophets and apostles whose writings would become canonical. We need to know where the church is going. We need to know the larger story of which we are a small part.

But, second, it is also clear that theories of church history always have an agenda. And since the church has suffered division internally and gone to war with other religions, the theories that emerge often require an enemy precisely where Christ commands us to see a sister, brother, or neighbor. One of the oldest and most destructive features of the Christian reading of history is seeing the Jews as eternal traitors, their false religion "superseded" by superior Christianity. The Pentecostal histories we have looked at briefly here require the Catholic church (and though they didn't usually know much about it, the Orthodox church, too) to be the bad guy. State and folk church Protestants have also often been identified as enemies. Of course, Lutherans and other Protestants did the same where Catholics were concerned, and Catholics regarding Protestants. Strikingly, the Charismatic movement in the historic churches has gone a long way toward healing the rift between them and Pentecostals.

In a certain sense, ecumenism is the church's self-inquiry on a grand scale of the meaning of its whole history: what early decisions remain mandatory today, what traditions can be safely discarded, how to take a canon of Scripture two thousand years old or more and apply it to the present. Ecumenism asks how we are to explain severe failures in the church—if indeed the Spirit really has been with us—and how we can knit our fragmented histories back together again.

As theories of church history go, dispensationalism and premillennialism are dangerous games to play. By definition they can't be subject to testing or argument. Oddly, even their most direct disproof, when the predicted end doesn't actually come, rarely seems to discredit them. They both require permanent conflict and the naming of other Christians as enemies.

Even more troubling is the fact that Christians are not the only ones to invoke dispensationalism, which leaves them quite vulnerable to dispensationalist exclusion by others. Islam understands itself to be a correction and replacement of decadent and confused Christianity. Baha'i understands every major religion in history to be a new dispensation replacing the previous one, and itself as the religion to replace the Islam that had replaced Christianity. Karl Marx believed he had unlocked the key to history in descrying the conflict between capital and the proletariat, with the new dispensation about to begin in the class conflict of his day. So did Francis Fukuyama in declaring capitalism to mark the end of history, which for him was praise, not criticism. Neither Marx nor Fukuyama foresaw the climate change crisis, which has made apocalypse a newly popular genre in the secular realm.

End-time predictions are pretty old, and so far none of them has been right. Of course, past failure is no guarantee of future failure. But instead of predicting either a far-off or a quite-soon end of the world, it is more helpful to think through the results of preaching and teaching one way or another.

When the church confidently asserts that Judgment Day is either non-existent or so far off that it needn't worry us, human thoughts and values can freely usurp God's. The church can continue on in blindness and complacency with no fear of reprisal. Terrible treacheries of the gospel ensue from such a mindset, ignoring Jesus' command to "keep awake."

On the other hand, many souls have been destroyed by self-appointed prophets and their fear-mongering about the end of the world. Livelihoods have been lost to those announcing an end that never came. If even the Son of God didn't know when the end would come (Mark 13:32), it's certain that no mere human being will. Predictions that claim to know the exact time and date are best distrusted and ignored. No one has the key to history but the Father alone.

It may happen that Jesus will come again in our lifetime, and it may not. But without any doubt, each of us will die and face Christ in judgment. There is nothing harmful and everything good in being prepared to meet him, confident that he is a gracious and merciful savior who loved us and gave his life for us.

For Further Reading

D. William Faupel, *The Everlasting Gospel: The Significance of Eschatology in the Development of Pentecostal Thought* (Sheffield: Sheffield Academic Press, 1996).

In the *New International Dictionary of Pentecostal and Charismatic Movements* (Grand Rapids: Zondervan, 2002), which is an excellent resource on Pentecostalism in general, see the articles on "Dispensationalism," "Eschatology, Pentecostal Perspectives on," "Latter Rain Movement," and "Restorationism in Classical Pentecostalism."

CHAPTER 8

Power

THE AZUSA STREET REVIVAL did not come upon unbelievers or non-Christians. It came to people who had already long since committed their lives to the gospel. But they felt something was missing. There was a dryness, an emptiness, a weakness in their faith and ministry. They looked at Scripture passages like Luke 24:49b, "Stay in the city until you are clothed with power from on high," and I Corinthians 2:4, "My speech and my message were not in plausible words of wisdom, but in demonstration of the Spirit and of power." They concluded that what they were missing was power. Not worldly power or even ecclesiastical power, but the power of the Holy Spirit.

Power came upon Pentecostals, and abundantly. The power of their witness has led to the most explosive growth in the whole history of the Christian church—and the only such growth entirely unaccompanied by military or government force. At the same time, paradoxically, power has been Pentecostalism's weakness. Power struggles have dogged its development every step of the way. Pentecostalism continues to deal with pastors and leaders arrogating power to themselves, arguments over the authority of prophecies and authenticity of miracles, and practices like the shepherding movement or deliverance ministries. Its enormous success has led many historic Christian churches and members to accuse Pentecostalism of proselytism: its power is perceived mainly as a threat, not as a gift.

This chapter treats a number of topics related to the exercise of power in Pentecostalism. Because power is such a pervasive concern, it shows up in many different areas and in many different ways. The topics covered here don't add up to a comprehensive study of the subject, but they offer a glimpse into this extremely complex arena and suggest some tools for discernment as readers encounter the many different manifestations of Pentecostalism.

Signs and wonders. While Pentecostals proclaim the Lordship of Jesus Christ, confess the Holy Trinity, teach that salvation is a gift rather than something to be earned, pray and sing and repent—just like all other Christians—the thing that other Christians are most likely to notice about them is their penchant for "signs and wonders." The more unusual charismata fall into this category, like tongues and prophecy, but so do all kinds of miracles, from healing to snakehandling to exorcism. Neocharismatics in particular, among them John Wimber and Peter Wagner, introduced in the 1970s the idea of "power evangelism." This is a method of earning the attention and ultimately the faith of unbelievers through demonstrations of spiritual power. But already in the nineteenth century, missionaries and missiologists had begun to give new attention to signs and wonders as central to the apostolic mission strategy. They had noticed that following the same apostolic pattern of wonderworking led to better results on the mission field. Signs and wonders were therefore linked with evangelism. They are not meant as ends in themselves but serve as conduits to faith in Jesus Christ.

The term "signs and wonders" (*sēmeia kai terata* in Greek) has a mainly negative connotation in the Gospels. Mark 13:22 and Matthew 24:24 use it to describe acts of power performed by false prophets and false messiahs. The Sadducees demand a sign (*sēmeion*) from heaven in Matthew 16:1, which does not earn a sympathetic response from Jesus, nor from Paul in I Corinthians 1:22. In John's Gospel, Jesus challenges a man who comes to him seeking a cure for his daughter with the words, "Unless you see signs and wonders you will not believe" (4:48). All the same, Jesus does as the man requests and heals the child. Throughout all four Gospels, Jesus heals, multiplies loaves, casts out demons, teaches with authority, sees into people's hearts and minds, and brings many to repentance and new life. These are indeed "signs and wonders," though even such extraordinary activity cannot force faith on anyone, as Mark 6:1–6 and Matthew 28:17 testify.

In Acts, "signs and wonders" has a much more positive connotation, whether applied to Jesus (2:22) or to the apostles (2:43, 4:30, 5:12, 6:8, 14:3, 15:12). The apostles heal, exorcise, and even raise the dead, drawing thousands to faith in Jesus, though they still meet with considerable resistance. Paul seems to have taken miracle-working for granted as part of his apostolic toolkit: "For I will not venture to speak of anything except what Christ has accomplished through me to bring the Gentiles to obedience—by word and deed, by the power of signs and wonders, by the power of the Spirit of God" (Rom 15:18–19a). The preacher who gave us the Epistle to the Hebrews wrote of the salvation that "was declared at first by the Lord, and it was attested to us by those who heard, while God also bore witness by signs and wonders and various miracles and by gifts of the Holy Spirit distributed according to his will" (2:3a–4).

The very idea of reintroducing or reclaiming "signs and wonders" today raises the question of authenticity: whether such things are even real. But the most controversial part of an already controversial practice is "deliverance ministry" or exorcism, which deals with evil spirits and seeks to release people from their control.

In point of fact, exorcism has always been part of Christian practice. The paradigm and justification for Christian deliverance ministry is Jesus' own exorcistic acts, as well as those of the apostles. Whether or not all the biblical writers assumed that Christians could and should engage in exorcistic ministry—Paul notably does not list it among the charismata—it is certain that all of them assumed the existence and activity of evil spirits threatening the world at large and Christians in particular. See, for example, Romans 8 on the powers and principalities, Ephesians 2:2 on the prince of the power of the air, Colossians 1:13 on the domain of darkness, II Timothy 2:26 on the snare of the devil, and I John 5:18 on the evil one. The exorcism of possessed adults has been at most a minor practice in Lutheranism, though Luther did give advice on how to go about it: calm prayer to God and assurance of gospel promises to the possessed were the main features. Up until the twentieth century Lutheran baptismal liturgies always included an exorcism. The "renunciation of the devil," which remains in many Lutheran liturgies to the present, is not the same thing and not an exorcism.

As should be expected by now, there is enormous variety among Pentecostals as to whether, when, and how to practice exorcisms. The general assumption is that any believer is capable of performing an exorcism, as long as it is done in Jesus' name and relies on the power of God. Charismatic Catholics, in keeping with the practice of their church, will generally turn to the appointed exorcist among the clergy. Most Classical Pentecostals insist that believing Christians cannot be possessed by a demon, though they might be oppressed or tormented by one. They and Charismatics alike will carefully distinguish between illness and demon possession.

Neocharismatics, however, will be more likely to attribute everything bad, including poverty and illness, to demons. (It's worth remembering that Jesus *both* healed illnesses *and* cast out demons.) This can extend even to character flaws, with the belief that there is a "spirit of laziness" or a "spirit of gluttony" or, in uppity women, a "Jezebel spirit." Sometimes they will commend self-administered exorcisms, often in the form of vomiting. The misleading term "authority prayer" is used by Neocharismatics for the command uttered by believers in Jesus' name to an evil spirit to depart from an afflicted person.

While people in the North and in older churches tend to react with skepticism, there is no question that a willingness to accept people's belief in evil spirits and battle them has been a major part of Pentecostals' success in the Global South. And where Lutheran and other historic churches have grown most rapidly in the South, they have also been willing to take up exorcistic ministries.

The most significant example of this is in Madagascar, a country with a long history of ancestor worship, traffic with the dead, and witchcraft. The Lutheran church's shepherding ministry of exorcism is credited with the church's rapid growth to millions of members. Specially trained and commissioned *mpiandry* or "shepherds" dress all in white, work in a team, and perform exorcisms during the course of a typical Lutheran liturgy. They begin with the recitation of four Bible verses authenticating their ministry: John 14:12–17, Mark 16:15–20, Matthew 18:18–20, and John 20:21–23. After a sermon, they walk among the gathered people, forcefully ordering the demons to depart in Jesus' name. Afterward they pray over individuals who ask for it, assuring them of forgiveness of sins in Jesus' name and asking Jesus for his healing in their life. This ministry is so effective that it has been adopted by the Catholic and Reformed churches, who have come to the Lutherans to learn how to do it. Similar, though less well-organized, deliverance ministries are also practiced by Lutherans elsewhere in Africa, in Asia, and more quietly in Europe, North America, and Australia, and not only by the Charismatics among them.

If there is one theme the reader takes away from this book, it should be the ongoing necessity of discernment—and there are no shortcuts to discernment. Some exercise of deliverance ministry is speculative, sensationalistic, and highly suspect. Creating maps of spiritual dominance by demons or blaming every flu or personality problem on an evil spirit goes well beyond anything the Bible authorizes and sometimes is just plain ridiculous. Demons should never become more interesting to us than the gospel!

At the same time, there is plenty of scriptural testimony as well as present-day evidence that some people do genuinely suffer from what can best be described as evil spirits or forces. Ministries of deliverance may help in releasing such persons from their oppression. It is as foolish to reject any of the weapons of the Spirit as it is to blame every single problem on the devil.

Post-Enlightenment Lutherans often forget or mock Luther's own teaching regarding the devil. In some cases, there is good reason for this: Luther was a little too quick at times to identify any enemy of his with Satan, failing to engage in the necessary process of discernment while justifying himself. But in his sober assessments he commended a practice worth remembering in times of extreme need.

To conclude this section: if the devil, demons, powers and principalities, or any other evil things exercise power in this world, then it is impossible for Christians to avoid responding in turn with the power of the Spirit. The danger is that even this power will be corrupted into something evil. Any attempt to battle the forces of darkness should be undertaken communally and collegially, never privately or individually, encouraging as much participation in the discernment process as possible and sharing the power granted by God for this end.

Leadership and Structure. As we have already had cause to observe, Pentecostals are not identified or united by a church structure, a liturgy, or a confession, but by a common experience. "Baptism in the Spirit" is what gave cohesion to the budding movement, not a teaching or church order. All the same, the power that Pentecostals experienced in their revivals needed to be directed and harnessed. Practical considerations demanded some kind of structuring: to accredit pastors and preachers and to protect congregations from false teachers; to organize missions and service projects; to disburse funds. In keeping with Pentecostals' restorationist impulses, they sought to shape their church structures in the way they thought was most faithful to the New Testament picture.

However, as restorationists always discover, it is hardly obvious what exactly qualifies as genuinely New Testament structures, since there are countless different interpretations! Accordingly, Classical Pentecostals and Neocharismatics have experimented with every possible form of church

government, from the rigidly episcopal to the independently congrega-
tionalist, from functionally presbyterian to nationally headquartered, from
relatively unstructured house churches to a virtually monarchical reign by
a single authoritarian pastor. Some Pentecostals appeal to the Ephesians
4:11 model of a fivefold ministry of apostles, prophets, evangelists, shep-
herds/pastors, and teachers (and thereby implicitly criticize the threefold
ministry of bishop, priest/pastor, and deacon in many historic churches).
Some value single-pastor oversight in a congregation, some prefer ministry
teams, and some call local pastors "bishops." Charismatics, for their part,
remain in and loyal to whatever historic model they have inherited.

One of the reasons for the great variety is that Pentecostals inherited
from Free Church Protestantism the conviction that the church is simply the fellowship of believers. Therefore, structure is to a large extent an
adiaphoron, a matter of indifference. The local congregation has always
been more important to Pentecostals than the regional, national, or transnational body. As we saw in the last chapter, Pentecostal beliefs about the
condition of the church through most of its history have led to a great deal
of skepticism about faith in the church as such. There is rarely any mention
of "the church" in Pentecostal statements of faith.

As is so often the case, Pentecostalism's strength in this regard is also
its weakness. Its minimalistic ecclesiology has meant an unprecedented
flexibility that allows it to adapt and grow in all sorts of new cultural envi-
ronments. This is one of the principal reasons it has long since outstripped
the historic churches in mission work. The latter have generally been so
concerned to preserve the accomplishments of their homeland that they
have lost sight of local needs. But at the same time, a general resistance to
mutual accountability and structured oversight has meant that less-than-
holy leaders and movements have been able to grow in Pentecostal fields
with almost nothing to check or limit them.

Thus, for example, Pentecostalism in North America is best known
to those outside the fold through corrupt television evangelists. A popular
preacher like Jimmy Swaggart gained an enormous following, only to have
his sexual misconduct discovered and publicized, discrediting his ministry
and that of other Pentecostals as well. Even more scandalous was the rise
and fall of Jim and Tammy Faye Bakker, Pentecostal TV personalities who
misdirected viewers' donations to support their lavish lifestyle, eventually
leading to the bankruptcy of all their institutions. Healing evangelist Oral
Roberts became famous for announcing that the Lord would "call him

home" to heaven if viewers didn't donate enough millions to support one of his projects. All of these men were affiliated with Pentecostal denominations but ignored the disciplinary warnings or simply left the denomination to go elsewhere. Success and wealth have often been more determinative of Pentecostal growth than accountability or authenticity.

The problem has existed at the other extreme as well. In the 1970s, a group of five leaders in the Charismatic renewal became convinced that what their movement needed was accountability to the maximum degree. They introduced the so-called Shepherding Movement (not the same as the one in Madagascar!). This required every single church member to "submit" to a shepherd/pastor, who would advise and control every aspect of the person's life, down to the most minute and intimate details. Male headship became an absolute value, too, requiring women to be utterly submissive to husband and pastor. Theoretically the shepherds were to practice the same level of submission, but the end result was a pyramid with less control the further up they went. Other Pentecostals and Charismatics attacked the movement for its alleged cultic qualities. In the end, the movement fractured because of growing tensions between the five founding leaders. Here again it is clear that an orientation to power attracts people to Pentecostalism while at the same time leaving it susceptible to corruption.

Of course, it is by no means obvious what form of church oversight or governance would guarantee safety from such problems. There is no ecclesiastical structure in the world that has managed to remain free of stain. But an orientation to power in church life does mean a particular susceptibility to the corruptions of power.

Unity. While unity in the Spirit is very important for them, unity in *structure* is not a primary consideration for Pentecostals and Neocharismatics —or a secondary or tertiary consideration either, and quite possibly not on the radar at all. As one Pentecostal ecumenist puts it, "the Pentecostal movement has managed, in just less than a century, to contribute to nearly as many different divisions as it took the rest of the church a millennium to produce."[1]

Most Pentecostals don't look upon that as a failure. If anything, Pentecostals make a positive good out of the decentralization of power. Their movement functions more like the internet than a pyramid—no hierarchy

---

1. Robeck, "Pentecostals and Ecumenism in a Pluralistic World," in *The Globalization of Pentecostalism*, 340–41.

per se but countless interconnections weaving a web of mutual relatedness. There is no central authority in Pentecostalism. The cost is that there are often local concentrations of power and authority instead. The fact that anyone is free to leave at any time without political or legal compulsion somewhat offsets the danger of this arrangement.

In the earliest days of Pentecostalism, power in the Spirit and unity in the Spirit were seen as very much belonging together. The earliest Pentecostals understood their movement to be above all an "ecumenical" one (though this is not the term they normally would have used). What the first Pentecostals experienced was a new work of God intended precisely to overcome the divisions within Christianity. Since Pentecostal fellowships attracted people from every existing strain of the Christian faith, it is no surprise that they interpreted their new movement in this way. Accordingly, it was of tremendous importance to them to insist that their new experiences were not driving them to create new *churches*. They were only a *movement* within and among the churches. No new constitutions were to be drawn up; no new creeds were to be composed; above all, no new barriers were to be erected.

This can be seen again and again in the extant sermons and newspapers of the period. In 1906, in the very first issue of *The Apostolic Faith*, the newspaper published by the Azusa Street Mission, the Pentecostal vision is described thus: "Stands for the restoration of the faith once delivered unto the saints—the old time religion, camp meetings, revivals, missions, street and prison work and Christian Unity everywhere. . . We are not fighting men or churches, but seeking to displace dead forms and creeds of wild fanaticisms with living, practical Christianity. 'Love, Faith, Unity' is our watchword."[2] Another early Pentecostal statement, from 1912, explains that "this is only a 'reform movement,' not a church, not the church, not the churches of God. As many churches as like can belong to this reform movement, as many do; but it is not a church, the church nor the churches; and it is a mistake we ought to get out of to call a Bible congregation of believers set in divine order by any sort of sector nickname."[3]

A few years later, a prophecy circulated among Pentecostals that attracted a great deal of attention and agreement. Speaking in the voice of God, it said: "I am seeking to draw my people together unto me. My people are scattered and are following many leaders. I am not pleased with that.

2. Quoted in Robeck, *The Azusa Street Mission and Revival*, 120.

3. Quoted in Vondey, *Beyond Pentecostalism*, 151.

Lo! I am the leader, and I want my people to follow me and not to be divided into sects."[4] Frank Bartleman, a prolific observer of the Azusa Street Mission and subsequent revivals, wrote: "There can be no divisions in a true Pentecost. To formulate a separate body is but to advertise our failure as a people of God. It proves to the world that we cannot get along together, rather than causing them to believe in our salvation. . . We had been called to bless and serve the holy 'body of Christ', everywhere. Christ is one and His 'body' can be but 'one'. To divide it is but to destroy it."[5]

It may well seem that this powerful unity was theoretical at most, even before the incipient Pentecostal churches began to divide over doctrinal and practical differences. It might sound like another variation on the "invisible church" theme to the detriment of the "visible unity" sought by the ecumenical movement throughout the twentieth century. This, however, is to miss the distinctive mark of the Pentecostal movement, which was most definitely visible: "baptism in the Holy Spirit." The unity of early Pentecostals was their unity in the shared experience of the outpouring of the Spirit. This event usually happened within the dimensions of corporate worship, and it gave rise to further corporate, unitive, visible signs: speaking in tongues, prophecies, healings, exorcisms. Even one hundred years later, the relative disinterest Pentecostals show in structural unity or even doctrinal unity is because they self-identify as Pentecostals on the basis of these visible signs of the Spirit's intervention in their lives. It has always been fairly easy for Pentecostals to cross denominational borders because of these visible signs of unity. Certainly it has been easier for them than for historic churches, which have made only slow progress through bilateral dialogues and fellowship agreements.

Still, Pentecostals have needed their own uncrossable borders to remain in place. Roman Catholics have always been the chief villains in the Pentecostal playbook, though historic Protestants have not generally fared much better. Along with Evangelicals, Pentecostals have often been all too happy to demonize "liberals" or "ecumenicals" for their betrayal of true biblical teaching. Sometimes the World Council of Churches has even been associated with the Beast of the book of Revelation!

---

4. Quoted in Robeck, "The Challenge Pentecostalism Poses to the Quest for Ecclesial Unity," in *Kirche in ökumenischer Perspektive*, 316.

5. Frank Bartleman, *Azusa Street* (South Plainfield: Bridge, 1925, reprinted 1980), 68–69.

That attitude is currently undergoing a dramatic shift, especially under the auspices of the Global Christian Forum. The idea for the GCF's creation came from Konrad Raiser, former General Secretary of the World Council of Churches, who realized that Evangelicals and Pentecostals would probably never join the WCC. The GCF was therefore formed in 1998 to create opportunities for Evangelicals and Pentecostals of all stripes to meet in a safe space with Catholics, Orthodox, and historic Protestants and have discussions about topics that were previously impossible to broach.

A particular topic of concern in the Global Christian Forum is dealing with accusations of proselytism and other abuses of power. Historic churches are seen by Pentecostals as using their longstanding cultural and legal status to protect their institutions and exclude others, even if they have failed in the ministry of gospel or have been complicit in political corruption. Pentecostals are seen by historic churches as poaching on another church's territory and disrespecting the serious challenges faced and met by these older churches. In any given situation, these accusations may have a grain of truth in them, or they may be overwhelmingly true on one side or the other or even on both.

As long as divided churches insist on seeing each other as rivals for a limited number of church members or converts, the disputes will continue. And as long as all churches seek to secure their own power—whether through legal precedent or sensational attractions—they will live at odds with the Lord who laid down his life for them, refusing the privileges of his own almighty power. A more excellent way is demanded of all churches that bear the name of Jesus Christ.

For Further Reading

Rites and Resources for Pastoral Care: Prepared by the Department of Liturgics Commission on Worship in the Lutheran Church of Australia, ed. David Schubert (Adelaide: Open Book Publishers, 1998) includes a rite of exorcism. The Lutheran Church of Australia's polity requires exorcisms to be performed only by bishops as a matter of accountability. See also the same church's statement "Authority and 'Power' in the Church," available online at <www.lca.org.au/doctrine-and-theology-2.html>.

Spirits, Ancestors and Healing: A Global Challenge to the Church: A Resource for Discussion, ed. Ingo Wulfhorst (Geneva: Lutheran World Federation,

2006) deals with some of the issues mentioned in this chapter and offers guidelines for discernment.

Lotera Fabien, "Healing Ministry of Ankaramalaza," *Africa Theological Journal* 35/1 (2015): 35–45 describes the shepherding ministry of the Malagasy Lutheran Church.

On Pentecostal ecclesiology and ecumenism, see the following: *Pentecostal Movements as an Ecumenical Challenge*, eds. Jürgen Moltmann and Karl-Josef Kuschel (London: SCM, 1996); *Pentecostalism and Christian Unity: Ecumenical Documents and Critical Assessments*, ed. Wolfgang Vondey (Eugene: Pickwick, 2010); Simon Chan, *Pentecostal Ecclesiology: An Essay on the Development of Doctrine* (Blandford Forum: Deo, 2011).

David J. Courey, *What Has Wittenberg to Do with Azusa? Luther's Theology of the Cross and Pentecostal Triumphalism* (Edinburgh: T & T Clark, 2015) is the fruit of a Pentecostal theologian's engagement with the theology of the cross to address problems internal to his movement.

Learn more about the Global Christian Forum at <www.globalchristian forum.org>.

CHAPTER 9

Prosperity

OFTEN WHEN LUTHERANS ARE asked what they know or think about Pentecostalism, their immediate reaction is a negative one. "Pentecostals are the ones who teach that if you're not healed, it's your own fault for not praying hard enough. They're the ones who say God will shower you with blessings—as long as you give the TV evangelist most of your money first. Health and wealth, name it and claim it—no thanks!"

This reaction is a perfect example of why ecumenism is so necessary to the faithful Christian life. There are indeed Christians who teach such things. But that message is not the original Pentecostal message. Prosperity has a much more complex history, with origins in nineteenth-century American metaphysical cults, picked up and propagated by an independent preacher named E. W. Kenyon (1867–1948) in the early twentieth century, and popularized by Nondenominational church entrepreneurs later in the twentieth century. The prosperity gospel has been rejected by many Classical Pentecostal denominations as well as by the historic churches to which Charismatics belong. But it is precisely because of prosperity's Nondenominational nature that it has made a big impact on Pentecostal and non-Pentecostal Christians alike. Prosperity's strongest holding today is in certain Neocharismatic circles but by no means in all of them, and you can sometimes hear prosperity themes even in the most historic of churches.

The result is that we must not equate prosperity and Pentecostalism. Rather, we must evaluate each church on the basis of its own teaching. This makes quick judgments extremely difficult, but we are better off that way. This chapter will therefore offer some historical background and theological tools to help Lutherans make those evaluations as necessary.

The first issue is terminology. There is no church that explicitly claims for itself the label "prosperity gospel." It is rather a critical term applied by outsiders. Quite often members and preachers of the prosperity gospel are not even aware that they are participants in a movement that has come in for severe criticism; it's just Christianity as they know it. If you come across a congregation with the word "blessing," "kingdom," "world," "victory," "champions," or "winners" in its name, chances are good you have discovered a prosperity church. Its members are likely to say they are part of "the Faith movement" or "the Word of Faith movement," or that they practice "Positive Confession." These names trade on solid Christian terms like "blessing" or "faith" but inject them with a very different meaning. That requires us to learn a basic lesson of theology: the use of the right *words* doesn't guarantee the right *teaching*. It's always important to study what the words mean to the people who use them, because it might be radically different from the way you use the words or the way the Bible uses them.

Next we turn to history. Prosperity arose in the optimistic setting of nineteenth-century America, where explorers and industry were conquering the earth by means of machines. The Christianity of this time and place, despite depicting America as the New Israel, was intensely individualistic, hosting revivals to foster dramatic conversion experiences and a personal assurance of salvation.

Industrial optimism and personalized religion collided in the metaphysical religions of Christian Science (a movement that denied the reality of the body and believed that all illness could be cured by pure mental effort), Transcendentalism (a unitarian philosophy that believed in the inherent goodness of human beings as opposed to corrupt society), and New Thought (a form of pantheism that claimed people were divine and could overcome all difficulties by right thinking). For the followers of these sects, it wasn't enough to conquer the earth and the body—one should above all seek to conquer the spirit. In fact, they usually believed that matter was only an illusion, while spirit was the one true reality. But spirit was as mechanistic as a machine. It operated according to certain immutable laws. All you had to do was figure out the spiritual laws, and then everything material you could ever want would be yours.

The aforementioned E. W. Kenyon grew up in such a religious environment. His only objection to New Thought and the other movements was that they weren't tied closely enough to the Christian faith. So he simply borrowed their logic and added some extra Jesus. For example, Kenyon argued that Jesus' death overcame all negative things in this life, including poverty and sickness. Thus, "faith" means taking advantage of the new spiritual law of victory in Christ. You couldn't just *hope* for something from God; you couldn't just *ask* for something from God; no, you had to *name* it and then you had to *claim* it—and as a result, it would be so. God was guaranteed to give it to you. As Kenyon put it in one of his many writings, "Christianity is a legal document."[1] If you sign on, God owes you; that's faith. Faith is a tool and a force to be wielded. Its words create reality just like God's did in Genesis 1, because Christians are little gods and supermen-in-the-making. Accordingly, one branch of the prosperity movement calls itself "Word of Faith," counting about 3.1 million official members today (but probably influencing a great many more).

A corollary of Kenyon's teaching was that physical signs are deceitful, distractions sent by Satan to lead you astray. Thus, a true believer suffering from illness simply asserts her victory over illness and from then on disregards the symptoms, which are temptations, not truth. Kenyon said that even to talk about illness was a form of devil worship. For this reason, some of the more extreme prosperity churches won't allow prayers for the sick, since that would be admitting to something negative and thereby making it true. While much of Pentecostalism is experience-driven, Kenyon's prosperity gospel is just the opposite: actual experience is to be utterly ignored, and the desired reality is to be confessed as already true.

Kenyon didn't become a widespread influence in his own time. He operated at the margins of church life. Many people have mistakenly assumed him to be a Pentecostal, though he was not. It wasn't until the second half of the twentieth century that Kenyon was rediscovered by other American evangelists such as Kenneth Hagin, T. L. Osborn, and Oral Roberts, who started popularizing Kenyon's thought (though not his name) through preaching tours and TV programs. Kenneth Copeland is the dean of such preachers today, but there are plenty of other popular prosperity leaders such as Creflo Dollar, Fred Price, and Benny Hinn. There are also Catholic versions of prosperity, such as the El Shaddai movement in the Philippines, which claims eight to ten million followers. Other prominent prosperity churches are the Yoido Full Gospel Church in Seoul, South Korea; the Hillsong Church in Sydney, Australia; and Igreja Universal do Reino de Deus in Rio de Janeiro, Brazil.

---

1. Quoted in Jacobsen, *A Reader in Pentecostal Theology*, 124. Jacobsen remarks: "Kenyon was never formally a part of any pentecostal church, and his view of the Spirit's work in the world is different from many other early pentecostals. . . It is probably best to think of Kenyon as a borderline figure, sometimes a pentecostal associate and at other times an outsider" (Jacobsen deliberately spells "Pentecostal" with a lowercase p).

Prosperity preachers are not organized into denominations or structures analogous to those of historic churches. But the term Nondenominational is nevertheless misleading in this case. Prosperity churches participate in networks of affiliation, some of which grant ministerial credentials to participating pastors. Examples of these are the Association of Faith Churches and Ministers, Creflo Dollar's Ministerial Association, and the International Convention of Faith Churches and Ministers. Networked pastors attend the same conferences, listen to the same speakers, and read the same books and magazines. Though there is no juridical structure to impose discipline, the voluntary association of such pastors and churches is nearly as strong in binding them together. There are also schools that train pastors who wish to associate with the movement, such as the Rhema Bible Training Center and Oral Roberts University, both in the state of Oklahoma in the United States. (Many faculty of Oral Roberts University, however, have spoken out strongly against prosperity theology.)

There is much to criticize about the prosperity gospel, but one word of caution must be spoken before we proceed. Prosperity has a very different impact depending on where and by whom it is preached. It is obviously repulsive when uttered by rich American preachers who extract life savings from naïve believers and then use the proceeds to fund an extravagant lifestyle. It is positively criminal when such preachers dissuade parents from giving their sick children the medicine necessary for survival, leading to an early and completely preventable death—as has happened far too often.

But prosperity is a popular message also in places that are not at all prosperous. It has a different texture when it is preached by and to people who are destitute, starving, and denied access to any medical care at all. In such situations, there is often a fine line between legitimate divine healing and illegitimate promises of believer-induced healing. Likewise, the message of prosperity can have the effect of pulling a marginalized community together. By supporting each other, people can create the stable economic and social relationships that allow the entire group to rise out of poverty.

Finally, many of the people who preach and practice the prosperity gospel are not aware of it as a distinct Christian movement with serious problems: it's simply the Christian faith as they've heard it. Discerning critics need to separate out the real flaws from the real benefits that have come to people through such preaching. And because of the loose networks of affiliation, it's often hard to say with absolute certainty who is and who is not really a proponent of prosperity gospel. It is more useful to be attuned to patterns of prosperity theology and practice that can appear in any church or preacher, whatever their official affiliation.

Here we will begin with a trinitarian approach to countering the claims of the prosperity gospel.

As we can see at the origins of Kenyon's teaching, there is a very faulty understanding of "spirit" at work. "Spirit" is made to be the enemy and the opposite of "matter," which is low, false, and unimportant. Such attitudes are very ancient. Christians have been fighting them since the earliest days of the church, whether in the form of Neoplatonism (a Greek philosophy of late antiquity elevating spiritual reality over material reality), Gnosticism (an early variant of Christianity that cultivated secret knowledge and despised the material world), or Manichaeism (a Persian religion that pitted the forces of good and spirit against the forces of evil and matter in an eternal struggle). By contrast, in the Nicene Creed we profess our faith in "the Holy Spirit, the Lord, the giver of life." This same Spirit hovered over the waters at creation and called matter, earth, and living creatures into being (Gen 1:2). This same Spirit raised up the crucified body of Jesus to new life (Rom 8:11): risen, transformed, but still a body, still something that could eat and drink and speak and even bear wounds. To be spiritual is not to be an enemy of the material.

And that means that we who live by the Spirit are called to be stewards of the material, not exploiters of it. The first task given to Adam and Eve, before they sinned, was to tend the garden and make the earth fruitful. But the prosperity gospel proclaims infinite greed to be rewarded with infinite accumulation, for the material world is purely an object to be used. There's no need to treat the material world with respect if it is inferior to the spiritual world; but if you enjoy material things, there's also no reason not to acquire as many of them as possible. Many prosperity preachers also assume that the return of Christ in glory is imminent, so there is really no reason not to exploit the planet in the meanwhile—after all, it won't last much longer. But the Holy Spirit created and sustained the world for the glory of God and for the flourishing of all, not for humans at the expense of the earth or for certain people at the expense of others. The psalms of creation (8, 19, 29, 65, 104, and 139) bear special testimony to this.

From the Spirit we turn to the Son. Prosperity preachers often assert that Christ already did all the suffering for us. Therefore, believers should expect nothing but success, victory, and wholeness. This is an extreme misreading of the whole testimony of Scripture, both of whose Testaments witness to the reality of suffering in the lives of the faithful. The book of Job is the most sustained biblical protest against the idea that those who suffer must be unrighteous—and equally against the idea that righteousness is a guarantee of happiness. Psalm 73 complains to God about the wicked: "always at ease, they increase in riches" (v. 12). Jesus was a shocking savior precisely because of his suffering on the cross. His earliest disciples and apostles shared the good news about this savior at great personal cost, even death. I Peter 3:8–4:19 discusses at length the suffering of faithful Christians.

Martyrdom has followed the faithful in all ages—and the last century saw more Christian martyrdoms than any other—but we are to understand martyrdom as a testimony to the faithfulness, not the failure, of God. As Dietrich Bonhoeffer, a German martyr under the Nazi regime, put it: "There are many Christians who bend their knees before the cross of Jesus Christ well enough, but who do nothing but resist and struggle against every affliction in their own lives. They believe that they love Christ's cross, but they hate the cross in their own lives. . . Whoever regards suffering and trouble in their own life as something wholly hostile, wholly evil, can know by this that they have not yet found peace with God at all."[2]

The most destructive thing the prosperity message does is convince people that, if they have not received the healing or wealth they have claimed from Christ, it is *their* fault. In such cases, there is no comfort for the bereaved, either: they can only assume that their loved ones failed and that's why the illness won. And prosperity preaching destroys the community. The wealthy are assumed to be the true believers while the poor must be doubters, so the strong are encouraged to cast off the weak in the name of holiness. Prosperity cannot endure the scandal of the cross. It cannot abide Jesus, the crucified savior of the world.

To reject the crucified Son is also to reject the Father Who sent him. In some ways it is understandable: human beings have always raged against their weakness and dependence, their vulnerability to suffering and death. Much religion now and throughout history is simply magic, an attempt to figure out the secret laws of the universe and exploit them for our own gain. Prosperity is twenty-first-century Christian magic. It wants control. It does not want a God Who is Lord over all, Who may call us to suffering for the sake of the gospel, Who cannot be explained or predicted or

2. Bonhoeffer, "The Secret of Suffering," in *A Testament to Freedom*, 290.

bribed. Luther identified this human tendency in Thesis 17 of the Disputation against Scholastic Theology: "Man is by nature unable to want God to be God. Indeed, he himself wants to be God, and does not want God to be God."[3] God is desired as a means to another end, not as the goal in Himself. Prosperity wants a God that can be bought off with "faith" or with generous giving in hope of an even bigger return in personal success—but does not really want *God*.

The Christian message does not take away the agony, frustration, or unanswered questions of human life. It doesn't promise victory or success right now. Instead, it declares that "the sufferings of this present time are not worth comparing with the glory that is to be revealed to us" (Rom 8:18). Jesus' vindication came after his death on the cross, when he was raised from the dead by the Father. So shall it be for us. To be a Christian is to share in the death and resurrection of Christ, not to avoid death or disdain the flesh that will be raised. In life and death and new life, the Father can be trusted to bring all things right.

Another critical approach can help in understanding and counteracting the prosperity message: a classically Lutheran law-and-gospel approach.

What does the gospel promise? Not health, not wealth, not a successful career or a solid marriage or a just government or happiness in this life. All of these things are good, all come from God, and all have their place—but in the law. The holy law of God is what governs our this-worldly life, directs us toward justice, curbs our sin, and reminds us of our constant need for God's mercy and forgiveness to get us back on track. The law teaches us to make good use of the gifts of creation and community through obedience and faithfulness. It is entirely appropriate for us to desire these good gifts of God; it is not even wrong to want to prosper.

So, to a limited extent, the prosperity message is right. Even Luther teaches that we are to turn to God in hope and prayer for every good thing, as we learn from the First Article of the Creed, for He is the source and sustainer of all. Endless misery, wrenching poverty, and crushing loneliness are not, after all, God's ultimate intention for any of us.

In the Old Testament, prosperity is promised, but—like all the promises of the *law*—it is promised conditionally. That condition is the keeping of the law and the covenant with God. For one example of many from Deuteronomy: "And because you listen to these rules and keep and do them,

3. Luther, "Disputation against Scholastic Theology," in *Luther's Works*, 31:10.

the Lord your God will keep with you the covenant and the steadfast love that He swore to your fathers. He will love you, bless you, and multiply you" (7:12–13). At the same time, the rules of the Torah and the prophets are preoccupied with the care of the poor, foreigners, the sick, and so on: "He executes justice for the fatherless and the widow, and loves the sojourner, giving him food and clothing" (10:18). In other words, from the Hebrew perspective, to seek one's own good *always and necessarily* entails seeking the good of neighbors and strangers. Wealth without social justice is an abomination in the eyes of the Lord. Prosperity preachers, by contrast, never stop to ask about the social, political, and ecological impact of the chosen few's astronomical wealth.

Moreover, the heartbreaking refrain of the Old Testament is that all of God's blessings showered upon Israel do not automatically result in Israel's fidelity to God. As long as we are sinners, prosperity can just as easily lead to wickedness and idolatry as to gratitude and righteousness. Again from Deuteronomy, a warning: "Take care lest you forget the Lord your God by not keeping His commandments and His rules and His statutes, which I command you today, lest, when you have eaten and are full and have built good houses and live in them, and when your herds and flocks multiply and your silver and gold is multiplied and all that you have is multiplied, then your heart be lifted up, and you forget the Lord your God, who brought you out of the house of slavery" (8:11–14). Again, prosperity preachers rarely stop to ask whether wealth might be a curse rather than a blessing. Our heart's desire might turn out to be a punishment.

For His part, the Lord finds Himself in a double-bind where prosperity is concerned. If He doesn't punish His people's evildoings by revoking the promised abundance, His holy law is made into a joke and the vulnerable suffer. If He does punish evil by taking His blessings away, the nations infer that He isn't God after all and further blaspheme His name (Ezek 36). As a result, and as countless Old Testament texts witness, prosperity and deprivation are visited upon Israel, and upon us, in a such a complex pattern—to say nothing of our own just or unjust attempts to control them— that simplistic assertions of either blessing or punishment can never be telling the whole story.

Prosperity theology thus distorts the biblical message with its half-truths. (Most heresies are wrong by being *partly* wrong, not *entirely* wrong. If they were entirely wrong, nobody would believe them.) Prosperity declares that good things come to those who deserve them, and bad things come to those who lack in faith or have done wrong. It is true, of course, that sin can lead to suffering. But God hardly needs to punish sins directly in this life: they tend to be their own punishment. To be an idolater is to be enslaved to a mute, dead, unresponsive thing instead of in a lifegiving relationship with the lifegiving God. Likewise, as Jesus said on the night of his arrest, "all who take the sword will perish by the sword" (Matt 26:52): violence begets more violence. The Proverbs warn that greed, abuse of the poor, laziness, and general unrighteousness will have severe consequences. God's good law is against sin, not least of all because sin is destructive of human beings and the whole creation.

However, we are not allowed to reverse this logic. Bad things, suffering, and disasters are *not* therefore always caused by sin. People tend to assume that suffering is always the result of evildoing, as a punishment. But Jesus forbids us to make that leap. He clearly stated that those who died in the collapse of the tower of Siloam were no worse than anyone else, thus their death was not caused by their particular sins (Luke 13:4). Likewise, the man was born blind not because he sinned or because his parents sinned; Jesus cuts off that interpretation entirely (John 9:3). Nor is abuse at the hands of other human beings payback for sin, for Jesus the sinless one was handed over to death on the cross. Quite often it is *righteousness*, not unrighteousness, that leads to suffering! The prosperity interpretation of suffering blasphemously distorts the law's good purpose of warning against evil deeds. Prosperity's interpretation of success also ignores the wrongdoing that often leads to wealth. For similar reasons Luther insisted that bearing the cross is a mark of the church, and he criticized the equation of success with God's blessing as the "theology of glory."

But we must return now to the question of what the gospel promises. The gospel is not either the created gifts of God or the law that protects them. And the gospel is not conditioned on our doing anything right, whether in obedience to God's law or in mastery of supposed spiritual laws. The gospel is nothing other than God's self-giving for us and for our salvation, purely gracious, purely on account of Who God is—a friend of sinners and lover of enemies. "God shows his love for us in that while we were still sinners, Christ died for us" (Rom 5:8).

Therefore, we are to love God for the amazing, unexpected, unearned gift of salvation above all—and not primarily for any other benefits we can get out of Him. As the eighteenth-century Icelandic pastor Jón Vídalín once preached: "[T]he same can be said about all prosperity pertaining to this life[:] Even at its peak it is often nothing but fraud and deception. Yet the fool worships it as a god; and even if he pretends to be God-fearing, he in fact loves the true God solely for the sake of such gifts as He bestows even on His enemies, and which conduce to their damnation when misused! I am afraid that those who love God only in hope of such perquisites do not love Him as they ought, even though He is certainly to be loved for everything that He gives."[4]

One more thing needs to be said, namely about how prosperity construes "faith." Lutherans should take special note, because prosperity relies on a terrible misunderstanding of a matter that was at the heart of the Reformation and the key to understanding all of our theology.

When Luther said that we are "justified by faith," he meant that we cease being enemies of God when we turn in trust, through the calling of the Holy Spirit, to Jesus Christ, who died on the cross for us and for our salvation. Faith, for Luther, is always a relationship, valuable more for Who it attaches us to—the triune God—than for what it is in itself. Faith is the end (or the beginning of the end) of sinful self-seeking. It is awaiting in confidence our resurrection to everlasting life with God and one another, trusting in Him to make all things right. That's why Luther could say, "If you believe it [i.e., the promise], you have it!" But for him such believing didn't work the way it does for prosperity preachers. For Luther, faith responds to the promise that God Himself speaks for our salvation. Faith is hearing, receiving, and believing that specific promise. It is not creating a new reality or exerting control over the universe, but accepting what God has done for us in response to His Word.

Ironically, "faith" in the world of prosperity is not faith at all! It is a claim for power, putting the believer in God's place to the point of idolatry. As Kenyon once wrote, "When these truths really gain the ascendancy in us, they will make us spiritual supermen, masters of demons and disease. . . It will be the end of weakness and failure. There will be no more struggle for faith, for all things are ours. There will be no more praying for power, for He is in us. . . In the presence of these tremendous realities, we arise and take our place. We get out and live as supermen indwelt by God."[5] Despite the appeal to God's presence in us, what Kenyon is really describing is a state in which we no longer need God at all.

4. Vídalín, *Whom Wind and Waves Obey*, 310.
5. Quoted in McConnell, *A Different Gospel*, 21.

That is not faith in the biblical sense. The Bible understands faith as a willing surrender of our lives into God's hands, acknowledging our dependence and gratefully enjoying our status as children of a loving Father. Another prosperity preacher, Fred Price, claims: "It's not God who heals you, it's your faith!"[6] But this kind of "faith" is not a relationship—it's a tool. God is not a Father but a bank to withdraw blessings from. Jesus' name is not that of our brother and Lord but a magic word to help us get ahead of everyone else.

Lutherans do believe that faith is a mighty thing. But it is not something we use to gain worldly benefits, and it is not something we wield like a weapon to control God. Faith is always a response to Christ crucified, which means that we also join him in his crucifixion. The victory of the resurrection is not an alternative to carrying the cross, but a hope that lies on the other side of the cross. "I have been crucified with Christ. It is no longer I who live, but Christ who lives in me. And the life I now live in the flesh I live by faith in the Son of God, who loved me and gave himself for me" (Gal 2:20).

For Further Reading

D. R. McConnell, *A Different Gospel*, updated ed. (Peabody: Hendrickson, 1994). McConnell wrote this study while teaching at Oral Roberts University. He demonstrates at some length the reliance of the original prosperity preachers like Kenneth Hagin on the metaphysical speculations of E. W. Kenyon.

Kate Bowler, *Blessed: A History of the American Prosperity Gospel* (Oxford: Oxford University Press, 2013) is the first history of the prosperity gospel.

One of the best theological statements against the false promises of prosperity, "The Believer and Positive Confession," was adopted by the Assemblies of God, the world's largest Classical Pentecostal denomination, in 1980, and is available online at <www.ag.org/top/beliefs/position_papers/pp.../pp_4183_confession.pdf>.

---

6. Quoted in McConnell, *A Different Gospel*, 94, fn. 20.

See also "A Statement on the Prosperity Gospel," Lausanne Theology Working Group, Akropong, Ghana, 8–9 October 2008 and 1–4 September 2009, available online at <www.lausanne.org/content/a-statement -on-the-prosperity-gospel>.

CHAPTER 10

Experience

As we draw toward the end of this book, it's time to revisit an observation made early on: that while Lutherans identify themselves confessionally, Pentecostals kinds do so experientially.

There is tremendous overlap between Lutherans and Pentecostals where doctrine is concerned. We together teach and believe in the holy Trinity, in the incarnate Son of God's death on the cross and resurrection, and in salvation as a gift freely given. But we do tend to differ on experiential matters. It could even be argued that our remaining doctrinal disagreements are organically related to our differing accounts of experience, because they center around issues related to the human will, original sin, and sanctification.

Lutherans tend to react to Pentecostals with the accusation of "Enthusiasm." This was the label given by Lutherans to other sixteenth-century reform movements that claimed to have direct knowledge of God apart from and independent of the Scripture. There is a great fear that Pentecostals are simply a new version of Enthusiasts, due to their emphasis on spiritual experiences, speaking in tongues, and prophecies. By now, hopefully, Lutheran readers will have seen that this accusation should not be applied to all Pentecostals without distinction, as an excuse to dismiss them. Some, of course, will prove to be modern-day Enthusiasts. But many and perhaps most will not. Once again, the rule is discernment.

On a theological level, it is more accurate to say that the real heart of the problem between Lutherans and Pentecostals lies in what each side believes is expected, promised, or possible for the human soul and the Christian life. So we need to wrap up this study with some reflections on the role of experience in Christian faith, theology, and church life.

One scholar explains Pentecostalism's approach to experience this way: "The movement's distinctive way of reading the New Testament leads it to the conclusion that, as in the early church, the modern believer becomes a disciple of Jesus Christ and receives the fullness of the Spirit's baptism in separate events or 'experiences.'"[1] The experiences available two thousand years ago are still available now. They are the very substance of what it means to be a Christian. Christianity is not so much a matter of belonging to a certain community, praying in a certain way, or adhering to certain beliefs. It is a matter of having a distinct set of experiences.

Pentecostalism arose out of the experience of "baptism in the Spirit" and the bestowal of charismata. These experiences were so determinative for the early movement that they became, in themselves, articles of faith. A certain *experience* became the object of *confession* and thus the glue that formed Pentecostals into a distinct Christian *movement*—and ultimately, a distinct *church* or set of churches or denominations. Theological interpretations of this experience came to dominate Classical Pentecostalism in the form of two doctrines: the doctrine of subsequence, which states that "baptism in the Spirit" is a subsequent experience to that of conversion (itself believed to be a distinct experience), and the doctrine of initial evidence, which states that a "baptism in the Spirit" can be verified by the experience of speaking in tongues.

So, for example, the Assemblies of God's Statement of Faith asserts in Article 7:

> All believers are entitled to and should ardently expect and earnestly seek the promise of the Father, the baptism in the Holy Spirit and fire, according to the command of our Lord Jesus Christ. This was the normal experience of all in the early Christian Church. . . This experience is distinct from and subsequent to the experience of the new birth. . . With the baptism in the Holy Spirit come such experiences as: an overflowing fullness of the Spirit. . . a deepened reverence for God. . . an intensified consecration to God and dedication to His work. . . and a more active love for Christ, for His Word and for the lost.[2]

The Statement includes supporting Bible verses, prominently featuring the Book of Acts.

---

1. Dayton, *The Theological Roots of Pentecostalism*, 24.

2. "Assemblies of God Statement of Fundamental Truths," §7, <www.ag.org/top/beliefs/statement_of_fundamental_truths/sft_full.cfm>.

The assumption at work is that Acts is not just history, not even just holy history, but a normative pattern or template that holds good for all the times of the church. Believers of any era should scrutinize their own experience in comparison with that of Acts. If the distance between them is found to be great, believers should seek to conform their experiences more closely to those found in Acts.

For Pentecostals, this approach did not arise in a vacuum or even from reading Acts. Rather, it started with their experience of spiritual dryness, their reception of astonishing spiritual power, and their search for an explanation. They identified their experiences with Pentecost, just as Peter himself had identified what was happening on that day with the prophecy of Joel, as he says in Acts 2:16: "This is that which was spoken by the prophet Joel."[3] Once the early Pentecostals had identified to their own satisfaction what was going on in their experiences, they drew doctrinal conclusions and extended them outward: all other believers can and should expect experiences similar to their own. Pentecostals' experiences went from being permissible and repeatable to being normative, bordering on mandatory. In Oneness Pentecostalism, these experiences actually did become mandatory for salvation. Yet in the end, they were defended not on the grounds of the experience itself but as a biblically proven doctrine.

This approach should sound familiar by now, especially in light of Pentecostal beliefs about church history and their restorationist impulse. Many Pentecostals (and other varieties of Protestants) have sought absolute consistency across all aspects of church life, attempting to design a perfectly New Testament way of ordering the church. However, there are other aspects of the Acts church that are not widely practiced by Pentecostals, such as holding all things in common (Acts 2:44) or selecting leaders by lot (Acts 1:26). There is always a principle of selection at work in attempts at restoration. Pentecostals have judged in favor of the normativity of their experiences of the Spirit, but they have not always considered other matters to be of such importance as to be reinstated in the same way.

Experience has proven to be a complicated and not always friendly standard for Pentecostals. The shared experience of "baptism in the Spirit" did not result in a harmonious movement or common conclusions about doctrine, church governance, and practice. If anything, quite the contrary. The liberating experience of "Spirit baptism" soon turned into another

---

3. From the King James Version of the Bible. "This Is That" is the title of the famous sermon by Aimee Semple McPherson, discussed in the chapter on history.

mandated article of doctrine that was disputed and divisive. Certainly not all Pentecostals, not even all Classical Pentecostals, ended up accepting the tongues-as-initial-evidence doctrine that has predominated in America. Despite hopes for a new revival, many of the Azusa-era Pentecostals criticized the Latter Rain movement of the 1940s just as fiercely as their own movement had been criticized a few decades earlier, denying the authenticity of the new revivalists' experience.

Here we see again that, among other difficulties with experience as a guiding light, is the second-generation problem of interpretation. Movements and churches always undergo a massive and painful shift when the original inspired leaders die and a new generation has to take up the torch. The first generation has the experience of conscious adult conversion, making the choice of something alien from its origins. The second generation, however, grows up from childhood already inhabiting the new belief system. The need to make a break with the past is simply not there. The situation is rather one of needing to mature in a belief always held (although, clearly, even first-generation converts need to go through a maturation process). New challenges start to arise in the second generation that were simply not on the radar of the first.

Think, for example, of the difference between the authentic Pauline letters and the Pastoral Epistles written by his heirs and followers. Or of the mighty battles fought in Lutheranism after Luther's death. Or even of the misunderstandings between immigrants and their "foreign" children. Pentecostalism, as an experientially-based movement, made sense to those who grew up in a Christian setting of spiritual dryness. But what about their children for whom charismata were not extraordinary at all? What about the second generation that had never known any Lord but Jesus?

A Pentecostal exegete, writing in the larger context of disagreements about baptismal practice, acknowledges the issue. "[I]t needs to be noted that the New Testament documents are for the most part all written to first generation adult converts and therefore simply do not describe or address the needs of the second and third generations. . . But for a second or third generation, who grow up in Christian homes, conversion is seldom so life-changing—nor, would I argue, can it or necessarily should it be so. But what happens is that the dynamic, experiential quality of the Christian life, as life in the Spirit, also seems to be the first element to go."[4] This intergenerational change invites serious reflection by all Christians. Why is "the dynamic, ex-

4. Fee, *Gospel and Spirit*, 118.

periential quality of the Christian life" the first to go? The question is itself an invitation to reflect on the historical experience of the church.

Biblically speaking, Pentecostals are right about this: the New Testament does *not* depict the Spirit as quiet, well-behaved, and barely noticed. The Spirit was, instead, unmistakably active, present, inspiring, and empowering. Experiencing the Spirit in this way, however, seems to be the minority report for most of the rest of church history. Even if Pentecostal attempts to offer a historical explanation are unconvincing and at times insulting to the historic churches, the need to offer such an explanation is not one that we can dismiss easily. All revival movements from Montanism to Pietism to Pentecostalism have sought to address the underwhelmingness of experienced Christian life. To make the unnoticeability of the Spirit a matter of doctrine, as seems to be unofficially the case in many historic churches, has more to do with the flat reality of church life than with actual exegesis of the New Testament. Christians who do not accept Pentecostal or Charismatic claims thus need to be aware how much their own arguments are based upon the *experience* of the church through history, not on the Scripture itself. There may be very good reasons for learning from the hard lessons of history, but there should not be any illusion about the fact that this is *also* a matter of experience, not an alternative to it.

One way that Pentecostals deal with the discrepancy is through their hermeneutic of experience. This hermeneutic extracts a set of mandatory experiences from the New Testament, based on the historical precedent provided there. It is the task of the church to identify and promote them; if the church fails to do so, then people will not have the necessary experiences. (This explains the absence of such phenomena during long periods of the church's history.) Both Pentecostals and Evangelicals teach a Christian experience of being "born again" at a specific time and date, which is equated with salvation. Pentecostals additionally teach Christians to expect a unique experience of "baptism in the Spirit," proven by accompanying charismata or a dramatically transformed life.

In either case, the assumption is that a true Christian passes through a definitive experiential order of repentance, faith, confession, water baptism, sanctification, Spirit baptism, and so forth. Experiences are codified, described, and preached so that others, not yet "saved" or "baptized in the Spirit," may yearn for them and be prepared for them when they happen. The experiencing of these experiences is considered sufficient proof that they are authentic. Still, most preachers in these communities are well aware of the problem of "backsliding," that is, of believers losing fervor or commitment to the faith. Another practical challenge is that the exact experiences and their order varies from church to church and denomination to denomination, undermining the conviction that an indisputable template of experience is to be found on the pages of Scripture.

There are parallels within Lutheranism. Some of the Lutheran Orthodox theologians, for example, tried to establish an *ordo salutis* or "order of salvation," diagnosing the various stages of repentance, faith, and regeneration. But, overall, less weight has been placed by Lutherans on defining and promoting a certain set of spiritual experiences as the content of the Christian life. Lutherans tend to place greater weight on Scripture's speech about *God* and His acts, rather than on its speech about *us* and our possibilities. The Lutheran hermeneutic puts the emphasis on claims about Christ, his person, and his work, while remaining modest about the extent of change in the human person. Lutherans do teach regeneration, but they deny that human beings can reach perfection in this life. Lutherans also do not expect that faith will be an absolute unwavering constant. This is why the task of the ministry is to preach God's commands and promises continually for the sake of inciting repentance, fostering faith, and guiding the new life in Christ. Luther put it nicely in one of his early writings: "This life, therefore, is not godliness but the process of becoming godly, not health but getting well, not being but becoming, not rest but exercise. We are not now what we shall be, but we are on the way. The process is not yet finished, but it is actively going on. This is not the goal but it is the right road. At present, everything does not gleam and sparkle, but everything is being cleansed."[5]

But as this very quotation shows, to reject experience out of hand is a half-truth, even when it comes to describing Lutheran theology. The question is not *whether* we will use experience, but *what kind of* experience we will use and *how* we will use it. Consider the example of Luther himself. When he had finally penetrated into the mysteries of St. Paul's Epistle to the Romans, he felt as though the heavens themselves had opened and he had been delivered from years of bondage. There is a very tight connection here between the hard-won understanding of Scripture and the personal experience responding to the truth of the new understanding.

Still, it is important to note, Luther then turned from Romans to the other books of the Bible, testing to see whether his new reading of Paul

5. Luther, "Defense and Explanation of All the Articles," in *Luther's Works*, 32:24.

matched up with other parts of Scripture. Luther further checked his experience against Augustine's treatise *On the Spirit and the Letter,* to find out whether his breakthrough had in fact been a breakdown. He was gratified and relieved to discover that the early church father verified his experiential breakthrough that itself arose from years of studying the Scriptures. In other words, experience helped Luther break through, but the experience was not conclusive in itself. It required testing against the experience of others and the whole biblical witness. Thus his famous remark recorded in the Table Talk, "[E]xperience alone makes the theologian,"[6] refers not to experience in general but to experience with the Scripture.

Accordingly, Luther offered guidance on what place experience should have in theology. There is the famous assertion from his 1520 commentary on Psalm 5: "Living, and even more dying and being damned, is what makes a theologian, not thinking, reading, or speculating."[7] His proposed method of Bible study was *oratio, meditatio, tentatio,* which means praying, then meditating, then finally being tempted or suffering through the work of the Scripture upon the soul. Bible knowledge was not something that people simply inserted into their brains and left there for safekeeping. It was an active transformation and sometimes an active torment, a decidedly experiential formation in the ways of God.

Furthermore, in the Heidelberg Disputation we find Luther's strong words about the theology of the cross and the theology of glory. Here he warns against a corrupt use of experience: namely, identifying the favor of God with what is strongest, brightest, most beautiful, most successful. That kind of experience would inevitably lead to a rejection of Jesus Christ himself. Rather, we are to recognize God's hand even in what is lowly, poor, humiliated, and downtrodden: the enslaved or exiled people of Israel, the young maiden Mary pregnant out of wedlock. This also became a principle for testing the claims of the "Zwickau prophets," who in the early 1520s claimed to have direct knowledge of God apart from the Scripture. Luther advised Melanchthon:

> If you should hear that all [their experiences] are pleasant, quiet, devout (as they say), and spiritual, then don't approve of them, even if they should say that they were caught up to the third

6. Luther, Table Talk No. 46, in *Luther's Works,* 54:7.

7. Luther, "Operationes in Psalmos," in *Luthers Werke,* 5:163, 28–29. The Latin reads, "Vivendo, immo moriendo et damnando fit theologus, non intelligendo, legendo aut speculando."

heaven. The sign of the Son of Man is then missing, which is the only touchstone of Christians and a certain differentiator between the spirits. Do you want to know the place, time, and manner of [true] conversations with God? Listen: "Like a lion has he broken all my bones"; "I am cast out from before your eyes": "My soul is filled with grief, and my life has approached hell". . . As if the [Divine] Majesty could speak familiarly with the Old Adam without first killing him and drying him out so that his horrible stench would not be so foul, since God is a consuming fire! The dreams and visions of the saints are horrifying, too, at least after they are understood. Therefore examine [the Zwickau prophets] and do not even listen if they speak of the glorified Jesus, unless you have first heard of the crucified Jesus.[8]

Later, in the Smalcald Articles, Luther argued that "[i]n these matters, which concern the spoken, eternal Word, it must be firmly maintained that God gives no one his Spirit or grace apart from the external Word which goes before."[9] All genuine Christian experience is a response to the prevenient act of God through His Word.

So, to give another test case of experience, this approach allowed Luther to judge in favor of priestly marriage. He and many other reformers of his time were confronted with the plain experience of priests struggling and more often failing with the celibacy required of them by the church. But their experience alone was insufficient to determine the case in favor of marriage; what was needed was confirmation by the Scripture. Luther indeed found that Scripture supported his proposed reform: "Now the Spirit expressly says that in later times some will depart from the faith. . . who forbid marriage" (I Tim 4:1, 3) and "If they cannot exercise self-control, they should marry. For it is better to marry than to burn with passion" (I Cor 7:9). This Scripture-informed response to experience became the basis for Article XXIII of the Augsburg Confession.

Experience has its role to play in contemporary Lutheran preaching, teaching, and pastoral care as well. The expectation is that, through the Christian ministry, people will *experience* the effects of law and gospel in their lives, being driven to repent and released for faith, joy, and new life. Experience is also why Lutherans insist so strongly on *simul justus et peccator*, "simultaneously righteous and a sinner." This formula is not found

---

8. Luther, Letter to Philip Melanchthon, January 13, 1522, in *Luther's Works*, 48:366–7.

9. Luther, "The Smalcald Articles," in *The Book of Concord*, 322.

in any direct form in the Scripture itself, and it is hotly contested by many other Christians. But Lutherans have experienced it to be true so many times over that any other conception of the Christian life is taken to be ideology, not theology—and, despite interpretative disputes, is found to be supported by Romans 7, among other biblical passages.

Thus, even Lutherans need to talk about experience, because theology and Scripture are not a *substitute* for human experience. Theology is not a safe haven up on a heavenly cloud that takes us out of the pain, confusion, and struggle of earthly life. Nor is it an ideology that says how things ought to be with utter disregard for how they actually are. If we were to disregard experience altogether, we would in effect be disregarding the entire creation—God's creation.

Perhaps it would be easier for those who shy away from the term "experience" to replace it with "history." Lutherans are generally comfortable talking about God's historical involvement in the lives of His creatures. But history is simply the long accumulation of human experience, from that of individuals to that of entire peoples and nations. Scripture is the record of Israel and the apostles' historical experience with God, an expansive experience that invites us to share in it. The scriptural canon offers a trustworthy guide to experience of God. Yet we are not only to *read* in Scripture about justification by faith: we are to *be justified* by faith! We are not only to *affirm* what the Bible says about the new life in the Spirit: we are to *participate* in the new life in the Spirit! The Scripture—as a report of human experience with the triune God—is one of the means by which the Spirit brings us to justification and participation in new life, as are the sacraments and Christian fellowship, among others.

Neither Scripture nor theology is a substitute for experience. They are, however, guides in the right interpretation of our diverse experiences. All experience is interpreted. Things don't simply happen to us in a chaotic, disconnected stream. Instead, we constantly seek to make sense out of what happens to us, stringing together a coherent narrative out of our lives. Left to ourselves, we would make a real mess out of our interpretations. Without the formative logic of the gospel, the rich and successful would assume they got that way out of their own particular merit; the poor and hurting would assume they did something wrong to deserve it; the wicked would infer that no punishment awaits their evil deeds; the righteous would doubt that God is just; and we would all be attracted to power and success but have no use for weakness, suffering, and the cross. The job of good theology is to *re*interpret our false interpretations of our own experience according to the real norms of the gospel of Jesus Christ.

Good theology also proposes other possible experiences, counter-experiences, to balance those that the world sends our way. These are the experience of prayer, the experience of the sacraments, the experience of the mutual consolation of the Christian faithful, the experience of love and self-giving, the experience of repentance and forgiveness; ultimately, the experience of God, through all these means. The encounter with Jesus Christ in the gospel is an experience in direct contest with the experience of sin, evil, and rival lords.

What about the other direction? Scripture and theology interpret and direct experience, but does experience interpret and direct theology and Scripture? This conversation has too often been arrested by disputes over whether any particular human experience can or should be normative for others. (One can easily see the eruptions between early Pentecostals and other Christians as being exactly this kind of dispute.) Therefore, let us assume that no human experience is normative for every other person. But let us then also acknowledge that we all have to live with the experience given to us—which for each of us personally, anyway, *is* normative—and that we all have to make sense of our own personal experience in the light of the gospel.

To put it more directly, we are entitled to the questions and tentative conclusions that our own life experiences force upon us. A resilient theologian will take up the challenge of personal experience and demand a good answer from theology. If theology has failed to do justice to that experience, then a theologian will press on and search and pray and scour the Scriptures until a better answer is found. Sometimes theology gets so profoundly stuck in a rut that only a flood of experience can set it free again. This happened, for example, in Apartheid South Africa, when white supremacist Christian readings of the Israelite invasion of Canaan and Romans 13 finally had to give way to the counter-experience of marginalized, brutalized African Christians who were reading Exodus, the stories of corrupt Israelite kings, and the interracial unity of the book of Acts. The same thing happened in the Reformation, when the huge dissonance between church tradition and the actual lives of Christians could no longer be sustained.

Experience therefore can suggest that something has gone wrong in the interpretation of Scripture. Experience cannot lay ultimate claims apart from Scripture, but Scripture sometimes needs the pressure of experience to be unlocked.

Experience likewise drives our ecumenical encounters. We may have no experience of the Christian other, or positive experience of them, or negative experience of them. Our experience of the other may be representative or it may be misleading. We may also misunderstand others' experience of us if we have in mind the ideal version of ourselves, but the other encounters the real (and definitely not ideal) version of ourselves. To give an example: some people leave historic churches for Pentecostal ones, left cold and empty by formal liturgies and attracted by the emotional force of more spontaneous worship. Others leave Pentecostal churches for historic ones, exhausted at the demand for emotion and comforted by the patterns and rhythms of the past. Neither preference is, in itself, right or wrong. The variety of worship speaks to the variety of human experience. Any ecumenical evaluation requires a careful study of the interplay of history, teaching, and lived reality—that is, experience.

We can see now that experience and Scripture coexist in the Christian life in a very complex pattern. Rather than suggesting stark opposition between Pentecostal and Lutheran approaches, this should encourage us all the more to join in dialogue about the discernment process in the interrelationship between the two. We have much to learn from and teach to one other.

For all Christians, the most important experience to which the Scripture testifies is the experience of God. God created the heavens and the earth, God delivered Israel from Egypt, God spoke by the prophets, God took on human flesh to serve, suffer, die, and rise again, God was poured out on Pentecost and many times thereafter to empower the apostolic ministry of the gospel. This God is true and real, the most true truth and the most real reality, more true and more real than any human experience of abandonment, persecution, sin, or evil. This God will triumph over the bitterest of experiences. This God will also triumph over false experiences of joy, such as those that come from the defeat of enemies or obsession with riches. No human experience can invalidate the gospel. But it will be God's business, in the end, to confirm His own promises and save His people. The gap in between is filled by faith.

Within this great and true reality that is God, the church and its people may experience a foretaste of divine fellowship while still on this earth.

This experience might come in humble and unremarkable ways, through the ordinary business of prayer and fellowship and singing and Bible reading. It may come in surprising and spectacular ways, through tongues and miracles and prophecies. It is good to recall here Paul's advice on the charismata: "All these are empowered by one and the same Spirit, who apportions to each one individually as he wills" (I Cor 12:11). Let there be neither envy nor judgment. These things are a matter of the Spirit's sovereign freedom.

But in preaching and teaching it is essential to be clear about what God *promises*. Salvation is promised to those who believe: "For God so loved the world, that he gave his only Son, that whoever believes in him should not perish but have eternal life" (John 3:16). The Holy Spirit is promised to those who are baptized: "Repent and be baptized every one of you in the name of Jesus Christ for the forgiveness of your sins, and you will receive the gift of the Holy Spirit" (Acts 2:38). There is no promise of God that every person will have a particular experience of any kind. Believers can be made aware of the possibilities of charismata and other experiences. But they can never be *promised* anything that God Himself does not promise.

Ultimately, every human experience, religious or otherwise, must be subject to the testing of the divine experience of the cross and resurrection of Jesus Christ. There is no greater wonder than the Creator and Lord of all humbling himself and becoming obedient to the point of death, even death on a cross (Phil 2). That experience is remarkable enough to fill us with wonder for all of eternity.

For Further Reading

Gordon D. Fee, *Gospel and Spirit: Issues in New Testament Hermeneutics* (Peabody: Hendrickson, 1991). Fee is a Pentecostal scholar of the New Testament who deals carefully and thought-provokingly with the heritage of Pentecostal hermeneutics in his book, especially in the chapters "Hermeneutics and Historical Precedent—A Major Issue in Pentecostal Hermeneutics" and "Baptism in the Holy Spirit: The Issue of Separability and Subsequence."

Ellen T. Charry, "Experience," in *The Oxford Handbook of Systematic Theology*, eds. Iain Torrance, Kathryn Tanner, and John Webster (Oxford: Oxford University Press, 2007), 412–31, offers a very sound approach to considering experience as a criterion in theology.

William Hordern, *Experience and Faith: The Significance of Luther for Understanding Today's Experiential Religion* (Minneapolis: Augsburg, 1983) is a good overview of Luther on the topic of experience while also engaging contemporary issues such as liberation theology.

In *The Book of Concord*, see Articles II, XII, and XVIII of the Augsburg Confession and the Apology of the Augsburg Confession on Original Sin, Repentance, and Free Will respectively, and the Formula of Concord I and II on Original Sin and Free Will respectively.

Conclusion

John said to him, "Teacher, we saw someone casting out demons in your name, and we tried to stop him, because he was not following us." But Jesus said, "Do not stop him, for no one who does a mighty work in my name will be able soon afterward to speak evil of me. For the one who is not against us is for us."—Mark 9:38–40

IN THE LIVED EXPERIENCE of the church, there are many conflicts, rivalries, and disagreements between different kinds of Christians. But as Mark 9 shows—along with so many other passages of the New Testament—all of us who call upon the name of Jesus Christ belong to him. And all of us who are baptized and believe in Jesus Christ also belong to one another. "But God has so composed the body. . . that there may be no division in the body, but that the members may have the same care for one another. If one member suffers, all suffer together; if one member is honored, all rejoice together" (I Cor 12:24–26). It is not a matter of us vs. them. What we do as Christians, how we preach and teach as Christians, affects other Christians. What other Christians do and preach and teach affects us. We belong to one another in the one body of Christ.

We also have a commandment from God: You shall not bear false witness against your neighbor. In the Small Catechism, Luther explains: "We are to fear and love God, so that we do not tell lies about our neighbors, betray or slander them, or destroy their reputations. Instead we are to come to their defense, speak well of them, and interpret everything they do in the best possible light."[1] All too often, Christians compete with each other and freely insult and slander one another. This behavior betrays the very word of God we have been given. It does not mean that we should never disagree, or that we should not rebuke false teaching when it is promoted. But it does

---

1. Luther, "The Small Catechism," in *The Book of Concord*, 353.

put the burden on us to speak truthfully, accurately, and charitably with and about our neighbors.

More positively, there is much we can learn from each other. While divisions are destructive, differences are not. No single community or theologian or tradition can encompass the whole range of Christian wisdom and insight. We may feel more at home in one church than another, but we can still grow and gain from the encounter with others. Pentecostalism has brought the whole church's attention once again to the dynamic presence of the Holy Spirit; to the contemporary possibility of charismatic gifts; to the vital importance of cultural adaptation and the prospect of a truly worldwide Christianity. We can further hope that Lutheranism's half-millennium of wisdom and insight may be of benefit to Pentecostals, though it is better for them to say what this might be instead of Lutherans informing Pentecostals of what they need to learn!

Regardless of theology or history or structure, the biggest felt difference between Lutherans and Pentecostals lies in their respective worship styles. Most often people judge other churches by the appearance of difference in worship, rather than by the substance of Who is worshipped and what is said about Him. We need to be more discerning interpreters of all liturgy and worship—both within our own church communities and without. And in the end, our goal should be the ability to join together in worshiping the one God our Father, Who sent His Son and gives His Spirit. So the final thing to say in this guide pertains to our ways of worship.

As a rule, Pentecostal services do not follow a historic pattern of worship familiar to the Lutheran tradition, whose own service was patterned on that of the medieval Western church. Pentecostal worship often seems disorderly and chaotic. This can be a misleading impression. It's more accurate to say that a *different* order is at work rather than *no* order at all. An hour of praise music followed by an hour of preaching concluding with prayer is itself an order. Sometimes "spontaneous" services are even more rigidly structured and consistently repeated week after week than traditional liturgies.

Some Pentecostal churches favor hymns in a style familiar to traditional Lutheranism, but contemporary praise music is overall more common. Often Lutherans dislike praise music for its apparent focus on "me," but this is also an often misleading impression. Much popular praise music is based on the Psalms, which are certainly full of "me" and "I"! The misinterpretation arises from the fact that Lutherans tend to think in declarative and instructive terms: hymns explain and announce the content of Christian teaching. Yet we too sing hymns declaring our own love, thanks, and faith toward God. Praise music's purpose is not, however, to *declare* how "I" feel about God, but rather to *form* the singer into a person who does indeed praise and worship God. It is performative, rather than declarative, speech. There is also often a progression in a set of praise music. Not everything is said in one song, but all the songs work together to present a broader view of the Christian faith.

The Lord's Supper is celebrated by Pentecostals but, in general, it is not given the same central importance that it has in Lutheran worship. As noted earlier, many Pentecostals came from a strongly anti-Catholic background and so simply adopted, without much consideration, the belief common in Reformed and Baptist circles that the Supper is a purely memorial act. This is a bit ironic, really, since Pentecostals' main conviction about worship is that "the Lord is present": present everywhere, apparently, but in the bread and wine! Some Pentecostal theologians have begun to reconsider sacramental theology along lines more amenable to Lutherans, and we may hope for mutual growth in this regard.

The Lutheran Confessions are quite strict on the matter of the Lord's Supper. They teach that "the body and blood of Christ are truly present and are distributed to those who eat the Lord's Supper" (Augsburg Confession X) and that the church is where "the gospel is taught purely and the sacraments are administered rightly" (Augsburg Confession VII). Yet while the Lutheran tradition is sacramentally strict, it is liturgically flexible. AC VII goes on to say, "It is not necessary that human traditions, rites, or ceremonies instituted by human beings be alike everywhere."[2] Liturgical decisions are to be made with regard to what benefits the community as a whole in coming to learn and believe the gospel. Thus Augsburg Confession XV states:

> Concerning church rites [the Lutherans] teach that those rites should be observed that can be observed without sin and that contribute to peace and good order in the church, for example, certain holy days, festivals, and the like. However, people are reminded not to burden consciences, as if such worship were also necessary for salvation. They are also reminded that human traditions that are instituted to win God's favor, merit grace, and make satisfaction for sins are opposed to the gospel and the teaching of faith.

2. Melanchthon, "The Augsburg Confession," in *The Book of Concord*, 45 and 43 respectively, Latin text.

> That is why vows and traditions concerning foods and days, etc., instituted to merit grace and make satisfaction for sins, are useless and contrary to the gospel.[3]

In order to be sure that the church's worship and preaching are purely and rightly carried out, the Augsburg Confession explains, the office of ministry was established by God.

It is worth noting, though, that the Augsburg Confession was written by Philip Melanchthon, who was not an ordained pastor! The office of ministry was not intended to limit or restrict the participation of lay Christians in worship, but to order it peaceably and make sure that it was really the *gospel* being preached and not some other word. Yet despite Luther's strong words about "the priesthood of all believers," for a variety of reasons the Lutheran tradition developed in a very clergy-centered way. Lutheran laity are often nervous about more active participation in worship, preferring instead to be silent except for singing the hymns and saying their responses. Many are frightened at the thought of praying aloud, even in private settings. Often it is only the pastor who has the opportunity to offer any unscripted speech in the worship service.

One of the reasons Pentecostalism has flourished, by contrast, is that it has given a voice to the voiceless. The liturgy is really "the work of the people," not only the recitation of the proper lines. Lutherans should be challenged to reconsider the interplay of right teaching through an educated and ordained clergy and the empowerment of the lay priesthood through more active participation in worship.

Nevertheless, the confessionally-approved flexibility in worship definitely does not mean complete license to do whatever we want. Luther's own approach to liturgical reform was very cautious. He wanted changes made gradually, with careful education of the people along the way, so as not to scandalize weak consciences. As much as he hated the canon of the mass (the part of the medieval communion liturgy that suggested the priests were sacrificing Christ on the altar), he was quite angry when it was simply dropped from the Wittenberg church's liturgy during his absence at the Wartburg Castle. The principle was correct, but the way it was carried out was loveless. Liturgical changes are to be made wisely, slowly, and considerately.

For, ultimately, it is worship that forms our faith and our desires. Worship gives us words to say to God and about God. Worship shapes our

---

3. Ibid., 49, Latin text.

attitudes toward our neighbors both in and out of the church. Worship captures our imagination with the stories and poems and laws and promises of the Scripture—or it fails to. Worship emboldens us to speak about the good news—or it keeps us silent. One of the oldest rules of the church is *lex orandi lex credendi*: the law of prayer is the law of belief, or, what you pray is what you will come to believe. All Christians of all kinds need to examine what they are praying and so coming to believe.

Do we pray to a Father absent from this earth, or one Who places His own name upon us in baptism? Do we pray to Christ the superhero, or Christ crucified? Do we pray to a Holy Spirit Who is invisible and unknown to us, or one Who is the very power of faith alive and at work in us? Do we instruct in God's law or only in culturally approved etiquette? Do we sing the whole story of salvation from Genesis to Revelation or only the parts we like? Do we proclaim divine possibilities or merely human ones? Do we preach God's promises or our own?

These questions invite extended and thoughtful soul-searching from all churches. They are better asked and answered in the company of other Christians than alone or in isolation. May we all be strengthened in the Spirit to seek out God's will for our communities and together proclaim the good news of Jesus Christ so that the world may believe.

Bibliography

Anderson, Allan. *African Reformation: African Initiated Christianity in the 21st Century.* Trenton: Africa World, 2001.

Assemblies of God. "Assemblies of God Statement of Fundamental Truths." www.ag.org/top/beliefs/statement_of_fundamental_truths/sft_full.cfm

————. "The Believer and Positive Confession." http://ag.org/top/beliefs/Position_Papers/index.cfm

Atkinson, William P. *Baptism in the Spirit: Luke-Acts and the Dunn Debate.* Eugene: Pickwick, 2011.

Bach, Eugene and Brother Zhu. *Crimson Cross: Uncovering the Mysteries of the Chinese House Church.* Blountsville: Fifth Estate, 2012.

Barratt, Thomas Ball. *In the Days of the Latter Rain.* London: Simpkin, Marshall, Hamilton, Kent, 1909.

Barrett, David D. "The 20th Century Pentecostal/Charismatic Renewal of the Holy Spirit, with its Goal of World Evangelization." *International Bulletin of Missionary Research* 2/3 (1988) 119–129.

Bittlinger, Arnold. *Gifts and Ministries.* Grand Rapids: Eerdmans, 1973. Translation of *Charisma und Amt.* Calw: Calwer Verlag, 1967.

Bonhoeffer, Dietrich. "The Secret of Suffering, Sermon at Finkenwalde, March 1938." In *A Testament to Freedom: The Essential Writings of Dietrich Bonhoeffer*, edited by Geoffrey B. Kelly and F. Burton Nelson, 289–293. New York: Harper One, 1995.

Burgess, Stanley M. and Eduard M. Van Der Maas, eds. *New International Dictionary of Pentecostal and Charismatic Movements.* Revised and expanded ed. Grand Rapids: Zondervan, 2002.

Chan, Simon. *Pentecostal Ecclesiology: An Essay on the Development of Doctrine.* Blandford Forum: Deo, 2011.

Charry, Ellen T. "Experience." In *The Oxford Handbook of Systematic Theology*, edited by Iain Torrance, Kathryn Tanner, and John Webster, 412–31. Oxford: Oxford University Press, 2007.

Christenson, Larry. *Welcome, Holy Spirit: A Study of Charismatic Renewal in the Church.* Minneapolis: Augsburg, 1987.

Commission on Theology and Inter-Church Relations of the Lutheran Church in Australia. "Authority and 'Power' in the Church." https://lca.box.net/shared/static/yhv6421d36kxh976sa5a.pdf

Courey, David J. *What Has Wittenberg to Do with Azusa? Luther's Theology of the Cross and Pentecostal Triumphalism.* Edinburgh: T & T Clark, 2015.

Cullmann, Oscar. *Baptism in the New Testament*. Translated by J. K. S. Reid. London: SCM, 1950.

Dayton, Donald W. *The Theological Roots of Pentecostalism*. Metuchen: Scarecrow, 1987.

Dunn, James. *Baptism in the Holy Spirit: A Re-examination of the New Testament Teaching on the Gift of the Spirit in Relation to Pentecostalism Today*. Nashville: Westminster John Knox, 1977.

Fabien, Lotera. "Healing Ministry of Ankaramalaza." *Africa Theological Journal* 35/1 (2015) 35–45.

Faith and Order Commission. *Baptism, Eucharist and Ministry*. Faith and Order Paper No. 111. Geneva: World Council of Churches, 1982.

———. *One Baptism: Toward Mutual Recognition*. Faith and Order Paper No. 210. Geneva: World Council of Churches, 2011.

Faupel, D. William. *The Everlasting Gospel: The Significance of Eschatology in the Development of Pentecostal Thought*. Sheffield: Sheffield Academic, 1996.

Fee, Gordon D. *Gospel and Spirit: Issues in New Testament Hermeneutics*. Peabody: Hendrickson, 1991.

Gaines, Adrienne S. "Study: Many Pentecostals Don't Speak in Tongues." *Charisma* (December 2006) 18.

Gritsch, Eric W. *A History of Lutheranism*. 2nd ed. Minneapolis: Fortress, 2010.

Hegertun, Terje. "Bridge over Troubled Water? Rebaptism in a Nordic Context— Reflections and Proposals." *Pneuma* 35/2 (2013) 235–252.

Holstrom, Bryan. *Infant Baptism and the Silence of the New Testament*. Greenville: Ambassador International, 2008.

Hordern, William. *Experience and Faith: The Significance of Luther for Understanding Today's Experiential Religion*. Minneapolis: Augsburg, 1983.

Jacobsen, Douglas. *A Reader in Pentecostal Theology: Voices from the First Generation*. Bloomington: Indiana University Press, 2006.

Johnson, Todd M. "Counting Pentecostals Worldwide." *Pneuma* 36/2 (2014) 265–288.

Knaake, J. F. K. et al., eds. *Luthers Werke*. Kritische Gesamtausgabe. 57 vols. Weimar: Böhlau, 1883ff.

Koenig, John. *Charismata: God's Gifts for God's People*. Philadelphia: Westminster, 1978.

Kolb, Robert and Timothy J. Wengert, eds. *The Book of Concord: The Confessions of the Evangelical Lutheran Church*. Minneapolis: Fortress, 2000.

Lausanne Theology Working Group. "A Statement on the Prosperity Gospel." www. lausanne.org/content/a-statement-on-the-prosperity-gospel

Lindberg, Carter. *Charismatic Renewal and the Lutheran Tradition*. LWF Report No. 21. Geneva: Lutheran World Federation, 1985.

———. *The Third Reformation? Charismatic Movements and the Lutheran Tradition*. Macon: Mercer University Press, 1983.

Luther, Martin. "Against the Heavenly Prophets." In *Luther's Works*, 40:79–223.

———. "Concerning Rebaptism." In *Luther's Works*, 40:229–262.

———. "Defense and Explanation of the All the Articles." In *Luther's Works*, 32:7–99.

———. "Disputation against Scholastic Theology." In *Luther's Works*, 31:9–16.

———. "Operationes in Psalmos." In *Luthers Werke*, vol. 5.

———. "The Large Catechism." In *The Book of Concord*, 379–480.

———. Letter to Philip Melanchthon, January 13, 1522. In *Luther's Works*, 48:364–372.

———. "The Smalcald Articles." In *The Book of Concord*, 297–328.

———. "The Small Catechism." In *The Book of Concord*, 347–375.

————. Table Talk No. 46. In *Luther's Works*, 54:7.

————. "To the Councilmen of All Cities in Germany That They Establish and Maintain Christian Schools." In *Luther's Works*, 45:347–378.

Macchia, Frank D. *Baptized in the Spirit: A Global Pentecostal Theology*. Grand Rapids: Zondervan, 2006.

McConnell, D. R. *A Different Gospel*. Updated ed. Peabody: Hendrickson, 1994.

McDonnell, Kilian, ed. *Presence, Power, Praise: Documents on the Charismatic Renewal*. Collegeville: Liturgical Press, 1980.

McPherson, Aimee Semple. *This Is That*. Los Angeles: Bridal Call Publishing House, 1919.

Melanchthon, Philip. "The Augsburg Confession." In *The Book of Concord*, 30–105.

Moltmann, Jürgen and Karl-Josef Kuschel, eds. *Pentecostal Movements as an Ecumenical Challenge*. London: SCM, 1996.

Nelson, E. Clifford. *The Rise of World Lutheranism: An American Perspective*. Philadelphia: Fortress, 1982.

"Oneness-Trinitarian Pentecostal Final Report, 2002–2007." *Pneuma* 30/2 (2008) 203–224.

Pelikan, Jaroslav and Helmut T. Lehmann, eds. *Luther's Works*. American Edition. 55 vols. St. Louis and Philadelphia: Concordia and Fortress, 1955ff.

Pew Research Center. "Global Christianity—A Report on the Size and Distribution of the World's Christian Population." www.pewforum.org/2011/12/19/global-christianity-exec/

————. "Spirit and Power: A 10-Country Survey of Pentecostals." www.pewforum.org/2006/10/05/spirit-and-power/

Pfitzner, Victor C. *Led by the Spirit: How Charismatic is New Testament Christianity?* Adelaide: Open Book, 1976.

Prenter, Regin. *Spiritus Creator*. Eugene: Wipf and Stock, 2001 (1953).

Rasolondraibe, Péri, ed. *Consultation on Renewal Movements in Lutheran Churches in North and South*. Geneva: Lutheran World Federation, 2002.

Robeck Jr., Cecil M. *The Azusa Street Mission and Revival: The Birth of the Global Pentecostal Movement*. Nashville: Thomas Nelson, 2006.

————. "The Challenge Pentecostalism Poses to the Quest for Ecclesial Unity." In *Kirche in ökumenischer Perspektive: Kardinal Walter Kasper zum 70. Geburtstag*. Edited by Peter Walter, Klaus Krämer, and George Augustin, 306–320. Freiburg: Herder, 2003.

————. "Pentecostals and Ecumenism in a Pluralistic World." In *The Globalization of Pentecostalism: A Religion Made to Travel*. Edited by Murray W. Dempster, Byron D. Klaus, and Douglas Petersen, 338–362. Oxford: Regnum, 1999.

Schubert, David, ed. *Rites and Resources for Pastoral Care: Prepared by the Department of Liturgics Commission on Worship in the Lutheran Church of Australia*. Adelaide: Open Book, 1998.

Vídalín, Jón. *Whom Wind and Waves Obey: Selected Sermons of Bishop Jón Vídalín*. Translated by Michael Fell. New York: Peter Lang, 1998.

Vondey, Wolfgang. *Beyond Pentecostalism: The Crisis of Global Christianity and the Renewal of the Theological Agenda*. Grand Rapids: Eerdmans, 2010.

Vondey, Wolfgang, ed. *Pentecostalism and Christian Unity: Ecumenical Documents and Critical Assessments*. Eugene: Pickwick, 2010.

Wulfhorst, Ingo, ed. *Spirits, Ancestors and Healing: A Global Challenge to the Church: A Resource for Discussion*. Geneva: Lutheran World Federation, 2006.

For more resources on Pentecostal and Lutheran Charismatic movements, please visit the website of the Institute for Ecumenical Research:

http://www.strasbourginstitute.org/en/dialogues/
lutheran-pentecostal-dialogue/

Subject Index

Abrams, Minnie F., 11
Acts, 8, 34–40, 42–47, 49–51, 53–57, 63, 77, 86, 92, 115–16, 123; *see also* Scripture Index
adiaphoron, 96
Adventists: *see* Seventh-Day Adventists
Africa, 12, 18, 20, 30–31, 94, 123
African-American, 3, 6–7, 14–15
African-Initiated Churches, 18
America: *see* United States of America
amillennialism: *see* millennialism
Anabaptist movement, 20, 54, 58, 79; *see also* rebaptism
Anglicanism, 10, 17, 20, 22, 31; *see also* Episcopalianism
apocalyptic, 87–89
Apology of the Augsburg Confession, 23, 126
apostles, 10, 28, 40, 45, 51, 55, 63, 65, 70, 75, 88, 92–93, 96, 107, 122
Apostolic Faith movement, 5
Apostolic Faith, The, newspaper, 1, 8, 98
Aroolappen, John Christian, 10
Arndt, Johann, 27
Asia, 94
Assemblies of God, 13, 115
Association of Faith Churches and Ministers, 105
Association of Vineyard Churches, 19
Augsburg Confession, 22–23, 25, 58n4, 80, 80n2, 121, 126, 129, 129n2, 130, 130n3
Augustine, Saint, 78, 81–82, 120
Australia, 21, 28, 94, 100, 104

authority prayer, 94
Azusa Street revival, 1–13, 16, 29, 49, 74, 91, 98–99, 101, 117

Baha'i, 89
Bakker, Jim and Tammy Faye, 96
baptism, believers', 3, 50, 54, 56–57, 59–60
baptism, by fire, 3, 11, 35, 85, 115
baptism, Christian, xii, 3, 7, 22, 27, 34–60, 64–65, 93, 117, 125, 127, 131
baptism, infant, 2–3, 31, 43–44, 50–51, 54–61
baptism, in Jesus' name, 8, 15, 37–39, 41–42, 44–45, 53
baptism, in the Holy Spirit, 3–11, 13, 15–17, 29, 34, 36–38, 42, 47–50, 52–54, 81, 83, 85, 95, 99, 115–16, 118, 125
baptism, in the trinitarian name, 7–8, 15–16, 58, 131
baptism, in water, 7, 22, 34–42, 45–46, 48–50, 53–55, 58, 60, 118
baptism, John's, 35–37, 39, 41–46, 49
baptism, of households, 43–44, 57
baptism, of Jesus, 35–36, 46
Baptist churches, 13, 19, 58, 129
Barratt, T. B., 82–85
Bartleman, Frank, 99
Bengel, Johann Albrecht, 29, 79
Bennett, Dennis, 16
Berlin Declaration, 29–30
Bible: *see* Scripture
Bible evidence: *see* initial evidence

Blumhardt, Johann Christoph, 29
Boddy, Alexander A., 50
Bonhoeffer, Dietrich, 107
Book of Concord: *see* Lutheran
    Confessions
Booth, George, 85
born again: *see* conversion
Brasil para Cristo, 19
Brazil, 18–19, 31, 104

Calvary Chapel, 19
Calvin, John, 20, 85
Catholicism: *see* Roman Catholicism
cessationism, 81
charismata, 18, 30–31, 35, 48–50, 62–77,
    81–82, 92–93, 115, 117–18, 125,
    128
Charismatics, Lutheran, 17, 30–34,
    75–76, 94
Charismatic movement, xi, 16–17, 19–20,
    30, 34, 87–88, 93, 96–97, 102, 118
Chile, 11
chiliasm, 78, 80
China, 18, 20
Christian Science, 103
church, xii, 22, 24–25, 34, 40, 45, 48,
    52, 54, 56–59, 62, 65–69, 71–75,
    77, 79, 82–84, 86–89, 91, 96–98,
    100, 102, 106, 110, 114–19, 124,
    127–29, 131
Church of God (Cleveland, Tennessee),
    4, 13
Church of God in Christ, 13
church order, 10–11, 13, 17, 19, 21–22,
    26–29, 32, 65, 71, 80, 95–97, 105,
    115–16, 128
Classical Pentecostalism, ix, 13–17,
    19–20, 30, 38, 48, 90, 93, 95, 102,
    112, 115, 117
commandments: *see* law
confirmation, rite of, 60
conversion, 2–4, 6–8, 10, 13, 15, 17, 27,
    29, 38, 40–42, 48, 57–59, 100,
    103, 115, 117–18
Copeland, Kenneth, 104
creeds, 23–24, 74, 98, 106, 108

Creflo Dollar's Ministerial Association,
    105
cross, xii, 8, 35–36, 41, 51, 75–76, 101,
    106–108, 110–12, 114, 120–22,
    125, 131

Darby, John Nelson, 80
deliverance ministry: *see* exorcism
Denmark, 26
Deus é Amor, 19
devil and demons, 23, 29, 41, 49–50, 69–
    70, 75, 93–95, 99, 104, 111, 127
discernment, 7, 59, 63–64, 69–71, 74–75,
    84, 91, 94–95, 101, 105, 114, 124,
    128
dispensationalism, 80–82, 84–85, 88–90
Disputation against Scholastic Theology,
    108
division, Christian, xii, 65, 71–72, 88,
    97–99, 127–28
Dollar, Creflo, 104–105
Durham, William H., 8, 13

Eastern Orthodoxy, 17, 22, 88, 100
ecumenism, ix, xi, xiii, 21, 60, 87–88,
    97–102, 124; *see also* unity,
    Christian
Elim Pentecostal Church, 14
elitism, 51, 65
El Shaddai movement, 104
empowerment, 6, 11, 30, 37–38, 40, 49–
    50, 52–53, 56, 65, 124–25, 130
Enthusiasm, 13, 51–52, 114
entire sanctification: *see* sanctification
Ephesian disciples, 44–45
Episcopalianism, 16, 31, 76; *see also*
    Anglicanism
eschatology, 2, 77, 80–81, 85–87, 90
Estonia, 26
Ethiopia, 30, 40, 54
eucharist: *see* Lord's Supper
Europe, xii, 2–3, 17–19, 26–30, 87, 94
Evangelicalism, 16, 25, 47, 58, 80, 87,
    99–100, 118
exorcism, 29, 75, 91–95, 99, 100; *see also*
    authority prayer

53–54, 56–57, 62, 77, 92, 95–96,
98, 131; *see also* empowerment
Mühlheim Declaration, 29
music, 1, 19, 24, 67, 69, 73, 125, 128–30
Myland, D. Wesley, 82n4

National Association of Evangelicals, 16
Neoapostolics: *see* Neocharismatics
Neocharismatics, 17–20, 31, 59, 87, 92,
94–95, 97, 102
Neopentecostals: *see* Neocharismatics
Neoplatonism, 106
new birth: *see* conversion
New Testament, 10, 33–34, 46, 50, 56, 60,
63–64, 74, 76–77, 80, 86–87, 95,
107, 115–18, 125, 127; *see also*
Scripture Index
New Thought, 103
Nondenominationalism, 18–19, 102, 105
North America, 14, 19, 28, 85, 94, 96
Norway, 26, 29, 82

Old Testament, 76, 107–109; *see also*
Scripture Index
Oneness Pentecostalism, 8, 15–17, 20,
116
Open Bible Standard Churches, 14
Oral Roberts University, 105, 112
ordo salutis, 119
Orthodoxy: *see* Eastern Orthodoxy
Osborn, T. L., 104
Ozman, Agnes, 5

Palmer, Phoebe, 2
Parham, Charles Fox, 4–8, 10
Paul, Apostle, 40–41, 43–45, 54, 56, 62–
68, 70–75, 77–78, 81–82, 92–93,
117, 119, 125
Paul, Jonathan, 29–30, 50
Pentecost, 4, 36–37, 39–40, 42, 49, 53, 99,
116, 124
Pentecostal Assemblies of the World, 15
Pentecostal/Charismatic Churches of
North America, 14
Pentecostal Church of God, 14
Pentecostal Fellowship of North America,
14, 85

Pentecostal Holiness Church, 4, 13
Peter, Apostle, 37–42, 51, 53, 55, 116
Philippines, 104
Pietism, 10, 27–31, 79, 118
Plymouth Brethren, 80–81
Positive Confession: *see* Word of Faith
movement
Postdenominationalists: *see*
Neocharismatics
postmillennialism: *see* millennialism
poverty, 63, 94, 103, 105, 107–109
power, 1, 5, 7, 18, 32, 36–37, 41, 48,
52, 62, 69–71, 82, 87, 91–100,
111, 116, 122, 131; *see also*
empowerment
power evangelism, 19, 92
power, political, 12, 22–23, 25–28, 45, 56,
73, 78, 91, 98, 100
prayer, xii, 1–2, 4, 6–7, 11–12, 30, 38,
40–41, 48, 53, 55–56, 62, 73, 75,
92–94, 102, 104, 108, 111, 115,
120, 123, 125, 128, 130–31
premillennialism: *see* millennialism
Price, Fred, 104, 112
priesthood of all believers, 130; *see also*
laity
promises of God, 37–38, 40, 43, 55, 77,
85, 93, 108–11, 114–15, 119,
124–25, 131
prophecy, 8, 10–11, 13, 31, 35–37, 42–43,
45, 49, 51–54, 63–67, 71–77, 80–
82, 84, 87–89, 91–92, 96, 98–99,
109, 114, 116, 124–25; *see also*
false prophets; Zwickau prophets
proselytism, 91, 100
prosperity, 19, 102–13
Psalms, 106, 128; *see also* Scripture Index

racial reconciliation, 1, 7, 9–10, 14, 52,
123
racism, 5, 7, 14, 16
Radicals: *see* Neocharismatics
Raiser, Konrad, 100
rapture, 81
Rauschenbusch, Walter, 87
rebaptism, 24, 45, 54, 57–61; *see also*
Anabaptist movement

Scripture Index

Luke *(continued)*

10:25–37	39
11:13	74
13:4	110
24:47	36
24:49	36, 91

John

1:33	35
3:16	125
3:22	35
4:2	35
4:4–42	39
4:48	92
9:3	110
14–17	64
14:12–17	94
20:21–23	94

Acts

1	42
1:5	36, 49, 85
1:8	37, 39, 49, 56
1:11	85
1:26	116
2	4, 6, 39, 56
2:4	6, 7, 14, 37, 49, 86
2:5–11	38, 42
2:16	116
2:17–18	51
2:22	92
2:33	49
2:38	37, 49, 125
2:39	55
2:43	92
2:44	116
2:47	55
4:8	54
4:23–31	53
4:30	92
5:12	92
5:32	49
6:8	92

8	39, 40, 56
8:12	38
8:14–17	38
8:17	49
9:2	40
9:17	40–41
10	41, 56
10:13	41
10:15	41
10:35	41
10:37	41
10:38	41
10:44	49
10:44–46	86
10:44–48	41
10:45	49
10:46	38
10:47	49
11	42, 66
11:15	49
11:15–17	42
11:16	49
11:18	42
11:26	40
13	70
13:24–25	43
14:3	92
15	42
15:8	49
15:12	92
15:14	40
16:11–15	43
16:25–34	43
16:30–31	43
17:28	68
18:24–28	44
19	44–45, 56
19:2	44, 49
19:6	38, 49, 86
19:9	40
19:23	40
22:4	40
22:16	44
24:14	40
24:22	40
26:18	85

148

149

II Timothy

2:26   93

Hebrews

2:3–4   93

James

4:2   74
5:14–15   14, 85

I Peter

3:8–4:19   107

II Peter

2:1–3   70
3:8–9   77

I John

1:1–3   70
4:1   51
4:1–3   64
5:18   93

Revelation

14   78
20   78, 80